BOMBING
AMERICA

The Deception
of the American People

Politics & Religion
Questions & Answers

ROGER H. EWING

ISBN-13: 978-1502339379
ISBN-10: 1502339374

Published by: Create Space

Printed in the United States of America

Formatting provided by Manuscripts To Go Book & Manuscript Services

Inspired by Emile Zola. The man who sought the truth. He fought for the successful exoneration of the falsely accused and convicted army officer Alfred Dreyfus. Emile Zola received 2 Nobel Prizes.

Roger Ewing is a seeker of the truth.

*Let us have faith that right makes might,
and in that faith let us to the end
dare to do our duty as we understand it.*

A Quote from Abraham Lincoln

Other Published Books

"Solving America's Debt and Deficit"
Published in May 2011

"It is Written — the Shocking
Downfall of the USA"
Published in November 2009

"Powerful Guide to Living the Good Life"
Published in December 1998
An Inspirational book

Subject of Master's Thesis:
"How to Solve a Problem"
Received an A+ from the University of
Southern California in 1970

You need to read the book from the beginning to the end to see how the "Bombing America" happened. It's an unbelievable story. But it was predictable.

There is a point of no return! It is the leaders of a nation that cause the point of no return. When the leaders' actions create chaos among the people because of their laws and executive orders than the people begin to not trust them. As the people begin to fear their government that point of no return is reached. This is especially true if a nation is founded on individual liberty and freedom. When a government starts taking away the people's individual liberty and freedom than a line has been crossed. This book attempts to address some of the issues that have caused fear among the people. This appears to be what is happening in the United States of America. A nation that the Founding Fathers gave credit to our Creator, Almighty God, as they realized that only through His hand the miracle of the United States of America was born. The Founding Fathers believed that God would watch over and protect America as long as most of the people believed and tried to follow His principles. That line has been crossed as the leaders and the majority of people stopped obeying the principles that made America the great nation it became. Woe to our elected leaders that have led to this evil that has beset us. The Judgment Day is coming!

In 1887 Alexander Tyler, a Scottish history professor at the University of Edinburgh, had this to say about the fall of the Athenian Republic some 2000 years prior, "A democracy is always temporary in nature; it simply cannot exist as a permanent form of government. A democracy will continue to exist up until the time voters discover that they can vote themselves generous gifts from the public treasury. From that moment on, the majority always votes for the candidates who promise the most benefits from the public treasury, with the result that every democracy will finally collapse followed by a dictatorship."

"The average age of the world's greatest civilizations from the beginning of history, has been about 200 years. During those 200 years, these nations always progressed through the following sequence:

From bondage to spiritual faith;

From spiritual faith to great courage;

From courage to liberty;

From liberty to abundance;

From abundance to complacency;

From complacency to apathy;

From apathy to dependence;

From dependence back into bondage."

Professor Joseph Olson of Hamline University School of Law points out an interesting fact concerning the 2012 Presidential election. Professor Olson said, "In aggregate, the map of the territory that Milt Romney won was mostly the land owned by the taxpaying citizens of the country. The territory Barack Obama won was mostly encompassed by those citizens living in low income tenements and living off various forms of government welfare."

"Olson believes the United States is now somewhere between the "complacency and apathy" phase of Professor Tyler's definition of democracy, with some forty percent of the nation's population already having reached the "governmental dependency" phase."

ARE AMERICANS IN DENIAL CONCERNING THE CONDITION OF THEIR COUNTRY?

Former President, Ronald Reagan, said," Freedom is never more than one generation away from extinction. We didn't pass it to our children in the bloodstream. It must be fought for, protected, and handed on for them to do the same, or one day we will spend our sunset years telling our children and our children's children what it was once like in the United States where men were free."

Thomas Jefferson said, "The democracy will cease to exist when you take away from those who are willing to work and give to those who would not."

John Adams said, "Our Constitution was made only for a moral and religious people. It is wholly inadequate to the government of any other."

On July 4, 1776, delegates to the Continental Congress voted to accept the Declaration of Independence in Philadelphia's Independence Hall. Fifty-six men signed their names to the historic document that gave birth to a new nation as they declared their independence from Great Britain. The men who signed the Declaration of Independence risked their lives, families, and fortunes for the cost of freedom.

Think of yourself, would you sacrifice everything for freedom?

When most of the leaders of a nation have faith in God than more people will follow resulting in a positive outcome. That's what happened with the signers of the Declaration of Independence. These signers are our Founding Fathers. But the cost of freedom to these brave men required enormous sacrifices. The following are some brief details that these men endured.

Carter Braxton of Virginia, a wealthy planter and trader, saw just about every shipping vessel in which he held an interest sunk or captured by the British during the Revolutionary War. During the war, he had loaned part of his wealth to support the war. The losses eventually resulted in great debt. As his debt grew, Braxton was forced to sell off his vast land holdings and the debt due him became worthless on account of the depreciation of the currency. In 1786, he was forced to leave his estate. He died in rags.

Thomas Nelson, Jr., of Virginia, raised $2 million to supply our French allies by offering his property as collateral. He was never reimbursed and he was unable to repay the note when it came due-- wiping out his entire estate. In the final battle of Yorktown, Nelson urged George Washington to fire on his home as it was occupied by British General Cornwallis.

Nelson's home was destroyed, leaving him bankrupt when he died.

Shortly after signing the Declaration of Independence, John Hart was elected to the new State Assembly and chosen its Speaker. When Hart left Philadelphia to take his seat in the state legislature at Princeton, he was besieged in his farmhouse during the invasion of New Jersey. Hart was driven from his wife's bedside as she was dying. Their 13 children fled for their lives. His fields and his gristmill were laid to waste. For more than a year he lived in forests and caves. He died from exhaustion and a broken heart.

On September 26, 1776, Richard Stockton was appointed to a committee to inspect the northern army. On his return home, he was betrayed to the British and was dragged from his home at night and taken prisoner in New York. Stockton was treated brutally. His home was destroyed and his lands ruined. Stockton never regained his health and fortune. He died in poverty.

Lewis Morris signed the Declaration of Independence even though he knew that a large British army unit had landed within a few miles of his estate and that his possessions would probably be destroyed. Soon after, his family was driven away, his livestock captured, and his entire property destroyed. Nearly all of his wealth was destroyed in the war.

Soon after Francis Lewis signed the Declaration of Independence, The British destroyed his estate in Whitestone, New York. His extensive library and his property were destroyed. His wife was taken prisoner for several months and was confined without a bed or a change of clothes. She died within two years after her release. Lewis having lost his fortune lived in poverty.

Arthur Middletown, Lyman Hall, William Hooper, Francis Hopkinson, William Williams, Button Gwinnett, and Thomas Heyward, Jr, all had their properties destroyed.

Five signers were captured by the British as traitors, and tortured before they died.

The courage and determination of our Founding Fathers and the signers of the Declaration of Independence often gets lost as we celebrate the 4th of July. We sometimes lose sight of the meaning of what INDEPENDENCE and FREEDOM mean. Do we have to lose our independence and freedom before we can embrace its true meaning?

To honor the signers of the Declaration of Independence their names are listed here:

Georgia -- Button Gwinnett, Lyman Hall, George Walton

North Carolina -- William Hooper, Joseph Hewes, John Penn

South Carolina -- Edward Rutledge, Thomas Heyward, Jr, Thomas Lynch, Jr., Arthur Middleton

Massachusetts -- John Hancock, John Adams, Samuel Adams, Elbridge Gerry, Robert Treat Paine

Maryland -- Samuel Chase, William Paca, Thomas Stone, Charles Carroll

Virginia -- George Wythe, Richard Henry Lee, Thomas Jefferson, Benjamin Harrison, Thomas Nelson, Jr, Francis Lightfoot Lee, Carter Braxton

Pennsylvania -- Robert Morris, Benjamin Rush, Benjamin Franklin, John Morton, George Clymer, James Smith, George Taylor, James Wilson, George Ross

Delaware -- Caesar Rodney, George Read, Thomas McKean

New York -- William Floyd, Philip Livingston, Francis Lewis, Lewis Morris

New Jersey -- Richard Stockton, John Witherspoon, Francis Hopkinson, John Hart, Abraham Clark

New Hampshire -- Josiah Bartlett, William Whipple, Matthew Thornton

Rhode Island -- Stephen Hopkins, William Ellery

Connecticut -- Roger Sherman, Samuel Huntington, William Williams, Oliver Wolcott

Chuck Colson wrote, "The references to God in the Declaration of Independence provide a foundation for a moral argument within civil society. And moral truths pervade our founding documents from beginning to end. Without God as the source of all those moral principles, the public square would quickly revert to the law of the jungle. Brutish power would prevail. Our nation's founding document declared independence from Britain, but with equal fervor, declared dependence upon God. Expressing "firm reliance on the Protection of divine Providence," the signers committed the American experiment to their Maker. The Spirit of 1776 was reverence and trust."

When most Americans do not understand what Independence and Freedom means then we as a nation are at a point of no return, we are lost as a nation. We have not only given up God but also the gift that He gave us. We need to learn history and remember why we became God's blessed people.

We have squandered our God given heritage.

History is clear what happens to a nation when its people turn away from God.

Remember Noah! The world had turned away from God. God was angry at mankind for all the evil in the world. He brought the floods that emptied the world of evil sparing only Noah and his family.

Remember Abraham who asked God to spare Sodom and Gomorrah. Those cities were destroyed for their sins. God has unlimited power. There isn't anything that God cannot do.

God is watching each and every individual twenty four hours a day seven days a week. How awesome is that! He is watching YOU!

God created the world and everything in it. As TIME passed, centuries passed, and man was "inspired" by God to progress with inventions that made life more bearable. This has brought man to the modern ages, where once there were mainly tribes now the world has nations capable of governing larger populations of people. But these nations all had kings or queens that ruled.

These rulers ruled with an iron hand. In time, in several of these nations people rose up to have more say in their lives, they wanted something which became called "individual freedom". But the rulers quickly quashed these movements. Why did these attempts at "individual freedom" fail? The author's guess is that the leaders of these attempts were not trying to create a nation that was built on Christian principles. History may have proven that "individual freedom" and Christian principles go hand in hand. You can't have one without the other.

But there arose a group of Christian men, who were mainly clergymen. History records that over half of the signers of the Declaration of Independence had studied at a seminary. These men were able to build churches of followers to live a life of Christian principles in a land that still was in its beginning. Depending on what historian one reads these Christian men were able to gather support of either 25% up to 33% of the population. Conditions were getting worse as the King of England established many laws, regulations, and new taxes until the moment came to stand up to fight. Inspired by God, an event, an opportunity was sitting in the Boston harbor and the Christian leaders understood and by their actions tea from the ship was thrown into the water. Even back then the British liked their tea and they didn't want it to be taxed. This started the American Revolution. In the author's opinion time and distance from England, which was the greatest nation in the world at that time, played a part in the success of founding the United States of America.

The war for "independence and individual freedom" began. Men swore their solemn oath, their fortune, and their life to the cause. Possibly two of the earliest men who became the most visible were John Adams who had written a letter published in a newspaper in 1764 and Samuel Adams who spoke to many church congregations both trying to wake up the colonists to stand up to the British king.

There were many prominent men who contributed to the cause. Of special note was the wise old Benjamin Franklin, the writer James Madison, the crafty politician Thomas Jefferson, John Hancock, Thomas Paine, and Alexander Hamilton.

The colonists had a MAJOR problem. That is an understatement! The colonists did NOT have an army and they did NOT have a navy. There were thousands of British troops in the colonies. These men had faith and trust in God that they could gain their freedom from the most powerful nation in the world. That takes a whole lot of faith! But nothing is impossible with God. Remember Jericho! How God instructed His people to walk around the walls of Jericho and how the walls miraculously came down.

The Founding Fathers asked George Washington who had some success in fighting the Indians to lead the Revolutionary Army. The call went out to men to join and form an army that would fight the British. Like today few men volunteered. It was risky to join an army that would fight the king. But those that signed up were trained to use a musket and learned the basic techniques of fighting. It was an army that had no money. Weapons were scarce, and boots and food were in short supply. Yet Washington did his best but lost battle after battle. Somehow more men heard about the idea of freedom and joined up. John Adams visited George Washington in New Jersey and realized the poor conditions of the men and the army. John Adams worked nonstop to get the supplies that Washington needed. And Washington miraculously won a battle. Word got out and more men joined. And they won another battle. They continued until they won the war. George Washington called it that God intervened with miracle after miracle. There was NO logical way to have won without God's intervention.

From the beginning of time as reported in the book of Genesis, God has stood by the nations that followed His word and served Him. The Israelite leaders, Noah, Abraham, Isaac, Moses, Joshua, and David for the most part obeyed God. And while they served God faithfully He brought favor to the Jews. But when they strayed, God allowed a punishment to the Jewish people. Amazingly, the Jews survived all the atrocities over thousands of years. The atrocities were for the most part self-inflicted because they stopped serving God and worshiped idols.

No matter how faithful one generation is, there will be a cultural crisis if the faith is not passed on to the next generation. Each generation needs to know God and follow His word. This was a major problem with the Israelites as many of their leaders didn't keep the faith to serve God. The United States of America has gotten into this same problem. We have lost our way in this country. It probably started back in the 1960s during President Lyndon Johnson's years in office. Up to that time about 80% of Americans believed in God and tried to live a Christian life. With the passage of Roe vs. Wade and the introduction of drugs people became more self-centered by looking for more self-gratification. Over 50 million babies have been aborted and hard drugs are easily accessible. And the First Amendment has been shattered as God has been taken out of our schools and society. As Americans gradually withdrew from God, God has gradually withdrawn from us. America has gradually declined over the last 50 years as less people served God. Depending on whose statistics one reads some report that only 35% to 45% of us truly strive to live a Christian life today. A look at the leadership in the United States Congress and our Presidential leadership one can easily understand why we are in this predicament.

How did the United States of America get into the predicament that we are in? America had a near perfect Constitution. Simply, the U.S. Senate, the U.S. House of Representatives, and the Presidents failed to obey the Constitution. They passed laws that had no foundation in our Constitution and the U.S. Supreme Court interpreted laws that eroded the meaning of the Founders and in essence wrote their own "legislation". Legislation is the sole function and purpose of the Congress, not of the Supreme Court or any court. PERIOD.

God's divine intervention was present with the men who wrote our Constitution. Over half of the signers were men who had attended a seminary. God was willing to work with the Founders as they knew His word and made an effort to create a document that expressed Christian principles and values. This was the first time in the history of the world that the governing document of a nation actually attempted such a feat.

George Washington said, "The Constitution will demonstrate as visibly the finger of Providence (God) as any possible event in the course of human affairs can ever designate it."

Daniel Webster said, "I regard the Constitution as the work of the purist patriots and wisest statesmen that ever existed, aided by Providence (God)."

In 2014, Is there ONE U.S. Senator that is a wise statesman? In fact has there been a wise U.S. Senator in the last 40 or 50 years? Unfortunately as a group today's U.S. Senators could be classified as one of the worst in American history. It is hard to predict if anyone in the U.S. House of Representatives will emerge as a wise statesman. Definitely the leadership in the House with Speaker John Boehner rates as one of the worst in modern times. Speaker Boehner and former Speaker Nancy Pelosi are two of a kind and history will judge them inadequate and inefficient.

The Constitution is the law of the land and it should be followed. How our leaders, past and present, have changed the meaning of what was written and what the intent was is appalling. For example, the First Amendment in reference to religion at that time of writing the Constitution was concerned about the

Church of England becoming the dominant church and religion. The Founders did NOT want any law that would have made the Church of England the religion of any state or the country. THAT WAS THE INTENT. The law was and is NOT to prohibit the free exercise of religion. The Congress and the courts have interpreted it to suit their own disbelief in God. Like in the days of the Jewish people worshiping idols these Americans have distorted the truth for all time and started the downfall of our nation. A nation without God is a failed nation.

Article 1, Section 1 of the Constitution states, "All legislative Powers herein granted shall be vested in a Congress of the United States, which shall consist of a Senate and House of Representatives." Therefore when Congress passes a law or defeats the passage of a bill the President of the United States cannot overturn the action by Executive Order. To do so puts the President above the law and acting as only a KING could act. One example of a President acting as a KING is Barack Obama as he has unilaterally changed the dates of several provisions to delay specific parts of the Affordable Care Act of 2010 from being enacted.

Article 3, Section 2 of the Constitution states, "The judicial Power shall extend to ALL CASES, in Law and Equity, arising under this Constitution, Laws of the United States, and Treaties made, or which will be made, under their authority." As we have three EQUAL INDEPENDENT branches of government and as the Supreme Court is the supreme court of the nation, why can't they act independently in taking up a case that is blatantly against the Constitution? Why must they wait for any length of time to receive a case from a lower court? Where in the Constitution is it written that they cannot do this?

In researching the terms "executive orders" and "federal regulations" it is almost impossible to define the AUTHORITY that is given to a President or a Cabinet Secretary. There is and has become a BROAD interpretation of the U. S. Constitution. A President can issue almost any "executive order" as he pleases. It requires three-fourths vote of the U.S. Senate to overturn an "executive order". Only twice in U.S. history have "executive orders" been overturned. In simple language, a President can rationalize that his "executive order" helps him to manage the country. A President can even involve the United States in a war by his "executive order" as President Clinton did in Kosovo.

A "federal regulation" issued by a Cabinet Secretary assumes that an Oversight Committee of the U.S. Congress is too busy to monitor and act what is actually happening in the country. Many of these "federal regulations" actually change the intent of a law originally passed by the U.S. Congress. A "federal regulation" has the same effect of being a law even as it is promulgated by unelected government officials. It is assumed that a Cabinet Secretary is acting on behalf of a President and has his authority. In fact a President can order a Cabinet Secretary to issue "federal regulations" as he sees fit. In essence a "federal regulation" could easily be seen as a President hiding behind a Cabinet Secretary.

Another distortion of power can be seen in the federal court system. A federal court judge can issue a verdict that changes a law that has passed the U.S. Congress or a law that was passed by a state. The INTERPRETATION of a law based on ideologically grounds of a judge or an administration can alter a law. The highest court in the land, the Supreme Court, in certain types of cases has original jurisdiction concurrently with lower courts. The original jurisdiction of the Supreme Court is governed by Article 3, Section 2 of the U.S. Constitution and Title 28 of the United States Code, Section 1251. It is the author's opinion that the U.S. Supreme Court should be the GUARDIAN OF THE CONSTITUTION. Therefore, whenever a President, a court, or any legislation, executive order, or federal regulation, GOES AGAINST THE CONSTITUTION the U.S. Supreme Court should act, take the case. If not what is their primary function? Under the U.S.

Constitution there are three branches of government, the executive, the congress (legislative), and the courts, if they are truly independent of each other why shouldn't the U.S. Supreme Court take up immediately any case or law that is unconstitutional? Why do they normally wait years before someone brings a case to a lower court and then wait more time before the case goes through the court system before they decide to take it? What if no one brings a case to a court or a lower court dismisses it on a judge's personal agenda? Does that result in an unconstitutional act that may never be heard?

The author has heard on television a number of times spoken by a U.S. Congressman that he does not have "standing" to file a lawsuit on behalf of his constituents if an unconstitutional law is passed that would harm them. In researching the legal term "standing" the author is not able to determine why a U.S. Congressman cannot represent his voters in a lawsuit. The legal term "standing" is defined as, "In law, standing or locus standi, is the term for the ability of a party to demonstrate to the court sufficient connection to and harm from the law or action challenged to support that party's participation in the case".

It seems that there is a maze of confusion and frustration built into the way the United States of America does its business.

What is the first priority of a President and the Congress of the United States of America? Inequality? Should the federal government take from those who work to give to those who do not? Don't think so. That is Socialism and that form of government has proven not to work. This should never be considered. Should affordable health care be our federal government's first priority? This is definitely worth considering but not as the number one issue.

What about climate change or as it used to be referred to, global warming? It appears the science has proven this as non-existent. Scientists say the last 17 years have actually cooled.

What happened to creating jobs? Definitely worth considering, but not priority one.

Whatever happened to national defense? Without a strong military that is capable of defending the United States every other issue is meaningless. We only have freedom because of our strong military.

FREEDOM IS NOT FREE! The ONLY thing that allows Americans to live the life of freedom is our military. Our military has fought to keep you and all of us free. Freedom, liberty, are not just words but a way of life. Our Constitution is not just words but a way of life that has been protected by our military. America has had to fight in wars in foreign countries to defend those countries and us from tyranny. If our military had not been up to the challenge of those wars we would be living more likely under a tyrannical government. The dictatorial countries of

27

Hitler's Germany and Hirohito's Japan had they won World War II the world today would be completely different. The American people rose up, joined the American military, and saved what was and is considered the "western way of life" and freedom.

The author will address the issue of our national defense later.

It's the Economy! The reader has heard this statement from our Washington politicians and President Obama over and over again. The old saying, "After all is said and done, much is said and little is done". How true this has been over the last five years.

Can the federal government grow the economy? Yes and no! If the federal, state, county and city governments employed half the people working would that grow the economy? That's about where we are today. Approximately half the American people are receiving a paycheck or check from government. The private sector work force pays for all the government checks. If the private sector stopped working or producing goods at a high level to sustain the economy, the economy would slow to a snail's pace. The economy grew at an anemic minus 2.9% for the quarter ending on March 31, 2014. This is the worst economic recovery since the Great Depression of the 1930s.

In 1979, approximately 63% of the population, those 16 and older, were working. In August 2013, 58.6% of the population, those 16 and older, were working, that's the employment-population ratio. According to the Bureau of Labor Statistics, a federal government organization, there were 90,473,000 Americans who did NOT participate in the labor force as of August 2013. In January 2009, when President Obama took office there were 80,957,000 who did NOT participate in the labor force. Approximately 10 million more people have dropped out of the labor force since January 2009. The BLS reported that 7.2 million worked part-time and another 2.3 million workers were "marginally attached" to the labor force. The "marginally attached" could be anyone who made ONE attempt during the last year to find a job. The "marginally attached" are NOT counted in the UNEMPLOYMENT figures. The total working force is somewhere between 150 million to 154 million, but subtract the 7.2 and the 2.3 million than the full time employment is around 140 million. If this is clear as mud to you, you are not alone. Just for the record the employment-population ratio in the United States has previously been 70%.

This is how Abbott and Costello explained the unemployment rate:

COSTELLO: I want to talk about the unemployment rate in America.

ABBOT; Good subject. Terrible times. It's 7.8%

COSTELLO; That many people are out of work?

ABBOTT; No, that's 14.7%.

COSTELLO; You just said 7.8%.

ABBOTT; 7.8% unemployed.

COSTELLO; Right, 7.8% out of work.

ABBOTT; No, that's 14.7%.

COSTELLO; Okay, so it's 14.7% unemployed.

ABBOTT; No, that's 7.8%.

COSTELLO; Wait a minute! Is it 7.8% or 14.7%?

ABBOTT; 7.8% are unemployed. 14.7% are out of work.

COSTELLO; If you are out of work you are unemployed.

ABBOTT; No, Congress said you can't count the "out of work" as the unemployed. You have to look for work to be unemployed.

COSTELLO; BUT THEY ARE OUT OF WORK!

ABBOTT; No, you miss the point.

COSTELLO; What point?

ABBOTT; Someone who doesn't look for work can't be counted with those who look for work. It wouldn't be fair.

COSTELLO; To whom?

ABBOTT; The unemployed.

COSTELLO; But ALL of them are out of work.

ABBOTT; No, the unemployed are actively looking for work. Those who are out of work gave up looking and if you give up, you are not unemployed.

COSTELLO; So if you're off the unemployment rolls that would count as less unemployment?

ABBOTT; Unemployment would go down. Absolutely.

COSTELLO; The unemployment just goes down because you don't look for work?

ABBOTT; Absolutely it goes down. That's how they get it to 7.8%. Otherwise it would be 14.7%. Our govt doesn't want you counted as unemployment.

COSTELLO; That would be tough on those running for re-election.

ABBOTT; Absolutely!

COSTELLO; Wait I got a question for you. That means there are two ways to bring down the unemployment number?

ABBOTT; Two ways is correct.

COSTELLO; Unemployment can go down if someone gets a job?

ABBOTT; Correct.

COSTELLO; And unemployment can also go down if you stop looking for a job?

ABBOTT; Bingo

COSTELLO; So there are two ways to bring unemployment down, and the easier of the two is to have people stop looking for work.

ABBOTT; Now you're thinking like an economist.

COSTELLO; I don't even know what the hell I just said!

ABBOTT; Now you're thinking like Congress.

This gets even more complicated with the health care law, Obamacare. As President Obama has delayed portions of the law over 30 times by his executive orders it is virtually impossible to come up with any true figures. Obamacare will transform one-sixth of the economy. The odds are there will be more negative numbers than positive numbers as it relates to the employment figures.

From January 2013 through July 2013, 77% of the jobs that were created were PART-TIME this according to Zero Hedge, a company that tracks these numbers.

Remember, the question was can the federal government grow the economy? Yes, by passing laws that allows the private industry to grow the economy. Yes, by stopping the federal regulations that hurt the private industry.

Obviously the numbers are not good, so let's take a look at realistically improving them. These are the author's ideas. This author likes to improve things and help with possible solutions.

Solution #1: As early as the 1970s this author stated that the migration of corporations shipping jobs overseas to China and other countries would one day hurt the American economy. This author was a management consultant to over 300 corporations in California. He has some idea of how business works and he also worked on his PhD in organizational development. So he has some knowledge of the practical and the theory. We have passed the point of no return as almost everything you buy today in the United States is made in China or some other foreign country.

So why did our corporations open manufacturing plants overseas, particularly in China? Simply, greed. Money, money, money, is a big incentive to grow a corporation's profits. The investors want more money. The CEO, chief executive officer, wants more money, as his salary and other compensation, bonus, perks, and golden parachutes have gone through the roof. The corporation makes a larger profit, and in some cases survives. But what did it do to the American workers who had good jobs in manufacturing? They lost their jobs. The manu-facturing sector of our country were the middle class jobs. If you were fortunate to work in manufacturing or one of the utilities you were in the middle class. But BIG business took their greed to a new level. Big business lowered their standards of quality to achieve even more profits. By allowing their products that did not meet American standards to be produced by foreign workers, especially those manufactured in China, they willingly accepted these lower standards. It's easy to say buy products MADE IN AMERICA, but they harder and harder to find. Now corporations are even putting DISTRIBUTED BY SO AND SO CORPORATION instead of putting where the product is being produced on their labeling. Wouldn't it be nice to see MADE IN AMERICA on products again? And wouldn't it be nice to buy QUALITY products again? Big businesses aren't the only ones to blame for creating our unstable economy.

We can also blame our Washington politicians. Why? They passed legislation giving corporations incentives to manufacture overseas. Yes, our representatives encouraged Big Business to open plants in China and elsewhere. We aren't going to change this as long as politicians want to be re-elected by getting donations from the corporations, big business. This is a politician's lifeline to continue in office. You see big business joins the Chamber of Commerce who lobbies the politicians through donations for their re-election campaigns and in turn the politicians enact incentives for these employers. Political campaigns have become very expensive. Anyone running to be elected to the Congress needs a ton of money. Advertising, especially television advertising, has become very expensive. Without television advertising a candidate's chances of winning are limited. The politician's greed of being elected or re-elected trumps everything else. It appears they, the politicians, lack of concern for the American workers and for America takes a back seat to their political ambitions. The American economy and the American worker will continue to suffer as long as big business, the Chamber of Commerce, and the politicians have it their way.

When it takes almost a TRILLION DOLLARS for a candidate to become President you know things are out of whack. It has been reported that's about how much Barack Obama had to spend in the 2012 election.

What is the solution? The solution is to put pressure on the politicians. Politicians by law are required to disclose the sources of their donations. Therefore, any politician who receives large donations from corporations or unions the voters need to vote against them. Second, during the campaign trail ask the politician if he/she will put a stop to corporations shipping American jobs overseas. Third, we need to elect the candidate who will work for the American worker. Fourth, then we need to get the politicians to stop the incentives for sending jobs overseas. Fifth, then the politicians need to step up and pass a law that puts an import tax on any American corporation or any corporation that has a relationship with that corporation. In order to stop the corporations, the tax should make it impossible for a corporation to make a profit by having a manufacturing plant overseas shipping their products back to America.

We need to find enough candidates who will do the right thing for America.

If the politicians put a 40% tax on American manufacturers that ship their products back to the United States that can and probably will require them to do one of several options. One, they can build plants in the USA to sell to the largest economy in the world which would require hiring workers. Two, they could use their plants overseas to just sell to the rest of the world. Three, they could close their overseas plants and sell their products to the USA and the world from their plants in the United States. If they don't build plants in the USA someone else will fill the void resulting in hiring workers. Either way the American economy will increase production in turn increasing jobs, This solution may sound drastic, but our work force and our economy needs this radical adjustment. If our economy can't sustain the growth needed to employ 70% of the eligible workforce to full time jobs than in time there may be chaos and even greater consequences. This solution along with the other suggested solutions will be full employment and even bring in more tax revenue for the government.

Another solution is to STOP the incessant dependency on COMPUTERS. Computers have taken over more jobs from people than any other tool.

Today manufacturing is highly dependent on computers. Robots and mechanical machines are programmed to do the work that people used to do. Technology is a wonderful thing if used in moderation. The problem with today's technology in manufacturing is that it is driven by greed, the almighty dollar. In other industries like communications and security it has crossed the line of individual rights and privacy. Is it time to require corporations by legislation to limit the use of computers to only one-third, 33%, of their production capacity requiring these employers to use people, human workers? This would not only affect manufacturing but all industries. Each industry has a capacity of work, or a production of work to which this would apply. American corporations must lead the way to restore the human workforce. The law would require that only those corporations, domestic and foreign, that comply to this mandate may sell their products in America. American corporations may not sell their products or services to any foreign country or corporation that does not comply to this new law. The penalty for American corporations not complying is the loss of all business licenses. This would apply to any foreign corporation doing business in America. Also, any foreign country that has any agreements or treaties, including security agreements, with the United States will become void if they do not enact the same law in their country. This is a worldwide phenomena that must be implemented in a reasonable time period so that no corporation or country gains an advantage.

Wouldn't it be nice to call a corporation and be able to talk to a real live person? Live telephone operators, that speak your language and that you can understand, use to be a great help to customers. Just think how this would RE-REVOLUTIONIZE the American and world economies. Millions of people would be hired with most of them being middle class jobs. An added benefit would be that workers would feel productive instead of just pushing buttons on a computer all day. Maybe we can have a happy work force again.

But this is just a utopian dream as Wall Street and other powerful individuals would fight this idea, but it is an idea that would help mankind which is not the goal of the powerful and the rich. And because the politicians receive their campaign money from the powerful and the rich this idea has a remote chance of success.

Another solution to help the economy grow can be to STOP MERGERS. The author has been against the largest or one of the largest corporations in an industry or even from another industry buying, or acquiring a competitor and then laying off hundreds if not thousands of workers. The only people who benefit from these mergers are the rich. Suggestion would be to compile a list of the top eight publicly traded corporations by assets in every industry and they would be untouchable for any merger. This could save thousands of jobs. Competition is the American way. Let the corporations compete.

One example of politics and power gone wrong is the city of Detroit. The city of Detroit was a wonderful booming city the envy of America. That was at the end of World War II, as American cars rolled off the assembly lines, the assembly lines that Detroit manufacturing perfected. Music companies thrived with the records of many of the big recording artists, many of the top singers of that time. But then something happened. In 1962, the people elected a Democratic mayor and the city council was dominated by Democrats. Detroit became a one party government. The one party government quickly instituted liberal policies including sweet deals for unions. From 1962 to 2014 there has NOT been a Republican mayor of Detroit. Liberal politicians expanded the city government and gave union employees what they wanted. So what happened to the paradise that was Detroit? The liberal policies and politics since 1962 wrecked Detroit. Taxes had to be increased to pay for the benefits that these policies created, benefits to the city government employees and union employees. Once great manufacturing companies struggled. But they found new hope as they built manufacturing plants in China where the labor costs were drastically lower. General Motors and Chrysler were bailed out by the American taxpayers. Detroit's population declined by 60% from 1960s high. Pension plans and health care plans which soared during the heyday suddenly became unmanageable creating large unfunded debts as more employees retired. Detroit filed for bankruptcy in July 2013. The top GM manager responsible for China said," General Motors was manufacturing about 70% of their vehicles overseas, mainly in China." GM hired thousands of Chinese workers, wonder what the unions think of this?

What do the top ten cities over 250,000 population with the highest poverty rate all have in common? The facts speak for themselves.

1. Detroit, MI. hasn't elected a Republican mayor since 1961 -- 32.5%

2. Buffalo, NY. hasn't elected a Republican mayor since 1954 -- 29.9%

3. Cincinnati, OH. hasn't elected a Republican mayor since 1984 -- 27.8%

4. Cleveland, OH. hasn't elected a Republican mayor since 1989 -- 27.0%

5. Miami, FL. has never elected a Republican mayor -- 26.9%

6. St. Louis, MO. hasn't elected a Republican mayor since 1949 -- 26.8%

7. El Paso, TX. has never elected a Republican mayor --26.4%

8. Milwaukee, WI. hasn't elected a Republican mayor since 1908 -- 26.2%

9. Philadelphia, PA. hasn't elected a Republican mayor since 1952 -- 25.1%

10. Newark, NJ. hasn't elected a Republican since 1907 -- 24.2%

It is the poor who habitually elect Democrats - yet they are still POOR.

Albert Einstein once said, "the definition of insanity is doing the same thing over and over again and expecting different results."

Henry Ford said, "Any man who thinks he can be happy and prosperous by letting the government take care of him had better take a closer look at the American Indian."

Abraham Lincoln said, " You cannot help the poor by destroying the rich. You cannot strengthen the weak by weakening the strong. You cannot bring about prosperity by discouraging thrift. You cannot lift the wage earner up by pulling the wage payer down. You cannot further the brotherhood of man by inciting class hatred. You cannot build character and courage by taking away people's initiative and independence. You cannot help people permanently by doing for them, what they could and should do for themselves."

When the U.S. Congress defeats a bill that the President wanted by what authority does a cabinet secretary have to issue regulations implementing what was in the defeated bill? The authority of a cabinet secretary comes from the President and both need to obey the Constitution. Also, the President cannot have a cabinet secretary issue regulations that he knows the Congress would defeat if he had attempted to pass as legislation. For example, the EPA has issued regulations on carbon that are stricter than the coal plants can adhere to. The technology has not been created to meet the standards imposed by the EPA. The coal industry has been forced to close almost a hundred plants laying off thousands of Americans. At the same time it has been reported by several news media that China is opening a new coal plant every week. The American coal industry has reduced their pollution by over 100% in the last 60 years. And coal is still the most dependable and cheapest form of energy. The United States has 250 years of coal in the ground that could and should keep our energy prices under control.

President Obama's push for GREEN ENERGY has cost the American taxpayers billions of dollars as much of the funding provided by him to green energy companies who have filed for bankruptcy.

The Obama administration provided loan guarantees and other federal dollars to companies that it hand selected. The Heritage Foundation put together a list of 34 companies President Obama's taxpayer backed green energy failures that received federal support from taxpayers that have faltered or are now faltering. These companies have either gone bankrupt, laid off workers, or are heading for bankruptcy. The list below provides the 34 companies along with the amount of money they were offered by the U.S. Department of Energy and other federal government agencies.

1. Evergreen Solar -- 25 million

2. SpectraWatt -- 500,000

3. Solyndra -- 535 million

4. Beacon Power -- 43 million

5. Nevada Geothermal -- 98.5 million

6. Sun Power -- 1.2 billion

7. First Solar -- 1.46 billion

8. Babcock and Brown -- 178 million

9. EnerDel's subsidiary Enerl -- 118.5 million

10. Amonix -- 5.9 million

11. Fisker Automotive -- 529 million

12. Abound Solar -- 400 million

13. A123 Systems -- 279 million

14. Willard and Kelsey Solar Group -- 700,981

15. Johnson Controls -- 299 million

16. Schneider Electric -- 86 million

17. Brightsource -- 1.6 billion

18. ECOtality -- 126.2 million

19. Raser Technologies -- 33 million

20. Energy Conversion Devices -- 13.3 million

21. Mountain Plaza, Inc. -- 2 million

22. Olsen's Crop Service and Olsen's Mills Acquisition Company -- 10 million

23. Range Fuels -- 80 million

24. Thompson River Power -- 6.5 million

25. Stirling Energy Systems -- 7 million

26. Azure Dynamics -- 5.4 million

27. Green Volts -- 500,000

28. Vestas -- 50 million

29. LG Chem's subsidiary Compact Power -- 151 million

30. Nordic Windpower -- 16 million

31. Navistar -- 39 million

32. Satcon -- 3 million

33. Konarka Technologies Inc -- 20 million

34. Mascoma Corp. -- 100 million

The above source was from an article on October 25, 2012 by the Institute For Energy Research which used the numbers from the Heritage Foundation.

This next list is from the Department of Energy Loan Programs Office dated May 8, 2013. It shows the loan guarantee and the number of permanent jobs created.

1. AREVA -- 2 billion 310

2. Georgia Power Company -- 8.33 billion 800

3. 1366 Technologies, Inc -- 150 million 70

4. Abenoga Bioenergy Biomass of Kansas LLC -- 132.4 million 65

5. Abenoga Solar, Inc. (Mojave Solar) -- 1.2 billion 70

6. Abenoga Solar, Inc. (Solana) -- 1,446 billion 60

7. Abound Solar -- 400 million 0

8. Caithness Shepherds Flat -- 1.3 billion 35

9. Cogentrix of Alamosa, LLC -- 90 million 10

10. Exelon (Antelope Valley Solar Ranch) -- 646 million 20

11. Granite Reliable -- 168.9 million 6

12. Kahuku Wind Power (First Wind) -- 117 million 10

13. LS Power Associates (SWIP-S) -- 343 million 15

14. Mesquite Solar (Sempra Mesquite) -- 337 million 7

15. Nevada Geothermal Power Co (Blue Mountain) -- 98.5 million 14

16. NextEra Energy Resources (Desert Sunlight) -- 1.46 billion 15

17. NextEra Energy Resources (Genesis Solar) -- 852 million 47

18. NRG Solar (Bright Source) -- 1.6 billion 86

19. NRG Solar (California Valley Solar Ranch) -- 1.23 billion 15

20. NRG Solar (Agua Caliente) -- 967 million 10

21. Ormat Nevada, Inc -- 350 million 64

22. Prologis (Project Amp) -- 1.4 billion 42

23. Record Hill Wind -- 102 million 8

24. SolarReserve (Crescent Dunes) -- 737 million 45

25. Solo Power -- 197 million 450

26. Solyndra -- 535 million 0

27. Stephentown Spindle (Beacon Power) -- 39 million
    14

28. U.S. Geothermal, Inc -- 97 million 10

TOTAL $26.32 BILLION 2,298

THAT IS $11.45 MILLION PER JOB

NOTE THE FIRST TWO COMPANIES ON THE LIST RECEIVED THEIR MONEY FOR NUCLEAR ENERGY. THEY CREATED 1110 JOBS OF THE 2298 JOBS CREATED.

IN 2008, BARACK OBAMA PLEDGED 5 MILLION JOBS OVER 10 YEARS BY DIRECTING TAXPAYER FUNDS TOWARD RENEWABLE ENERGY PROJECTS. WITH ONLY 2 THOUSAND 2 HUNDRED 98 JOBS CREATED, HE IS FAR SHORT OF THE GOAL.

The American public has become immune to certain words as they have heard them over and over again and again to the point that they don't register anymore the extent of their meaning. For example, politicians used to talk about "millions" but have progressed to "billions" of dollars for their programs. The next time you hear a politician use the word "billion" in a casual manner think about this. To help you better understand a "billion" here are some thoughts:

A BILLION SECONDS AGO IT WAS 1959.

A BILLION MINUTES AGO JESUS WAS ALIVE.

A BILLION HOURS AGO OUR ANCESTORS WERE LIVING IN THE STONE AGE.

A BILLION DAYS AGO NO ONE WALKED ON THE EARTH ON TWO FEET.

A BILLION DOLLARS AGO WAS ONLY 8 HOURS AND TWENTY MINUTES AT THE RATE OUR GOVERNMENT IS SPENDING.

Now "trillion" of dollars is thrown around by some politicians as the new norm.

When Barack Obama became President in January 2009 the national debt was about $10.6 trillion dollars. Since he has been in office the national debt has increased to over $17.5 trillion dollars, a 60% increase. By the end of 2016, the end of Barack Obama's second term, it is estimated that the national debt will be $20 trillion dollars.

The burden of debt is as destructive to freedom as subjugation by conquest. In fact, history as proven that over and over again. Woe to every politician who had a hand in creating this enormous debt to our nation. It is written there is a judgment day. Therefore, any politician who voted their political party preferences over the good of our nation will answer for their selfish and cowardly deeds. God forgives a person's sin in his/her private life but the sin a person commits as a representative of the people HE will deal with based on the enormity of the sin.

Americans have been deceived by our politicians for years. They have been in denial or just plain apathetic about the direction our nation is going.

In Exodus 18:21, "Moreover thou shalt provide out of all the people able men, such as fear God, men of truth, hating covetous: and place such over them, to be rulers."

In Chronicles 7:14, "If my people, which are called by my name, shall humble themselves, and pray, and seek my face, and turn from their wicked ways: then will I hear from heaven, and forgive their sin, and heal their land.

The national debt of the United States is the composite of many sins. First, the politicians who got us in the mess we are in. Second, to the people who have the power to make decisions, those elected and those not elected but those with influence. Third, to the judges who defiled our Constitution. Fourth, to the people who did not educate themselves to pay attention to the government failings. Fifth, to anyone who has taken money under false pretense from the government. Sixth, to the wealthy donors to election campaigns who supported candidates who were unworthy based on their prior unconstitutional voting records. Seventh, to anyone who has spread false teachings about the Word of God.

Are we at a point of no return? Jesus said we need to turn from our wicked ways. America WAS the sacred nation, protected by Almighty God. Now we are on our own as only about 40% of the people even try to live according to the principles of the Bible. God didn't change, we did. Unfaithfulness to God begets evil. History is filled with examples of what happens to nations when they turn from God.

Let's look at the deception of wind power. John Droz, Jr. a physicist and environmental advocate, has researched wind power and has written the following. This is a quick highlight review of how things have evolved with wind merchandising.

Wind energy was abandoned well over a hundred years ago, as even in the late 1800s it was totally inconsistent with our burgeoning more modern needs for power. When we throw the switch, we expect that the lights will go on. - 100% of the time. It's not possible for wind energy, by itself, to EVER do this which is one of the main reasons it was relegated to the dust bin of antiquated technologies along with such other inadequate energy sources as horse and oxen power.

Fast forward to several years ago. With politicians being convinced that Anthropogenic Global Warning (AGW) was an imminent catastrophic threat, lobbyists launched campaigns to favor anything that would purportedly reduce carbon dioxide. This was the marketing opportunity that the wind energy business needed. Wind energy was resurrected from the dust bin of power sources, as its promoters pushed the fact that wind turbines did not produce CO_2 while generating electricity.

Of course, just that by itself is not significant, so the original wind development lobbyists then made the case for a quantum leap: that by adding wind turbines to the grid we could significantly reduce CO_2 from those "dirty" fossil fuel electrical sources especially coal. This argument became the basis for many states implementing a Renewable Energy Standard (RES) or Renewable Portfolio Standard (RPS) which mandated that the states' utilities use or purchase a prescribed amount of wind energy (renewables) by a set date.

Why was a mandate necessary? Simply because the real world reality of integrating wind energy made it a very expensive option. As such, no utility companies would likely do so on their own. They had to be forced to.

Interestingly, although the stated main goal of these RES/RPS programs was to reduce CO_2, not a single state's RES/RPS requires VERIFICATION of CO_2 reduction from any wind project, either beforehand or after the fact. The politicians simply took the sales peoples' word that consequential CO_2 savings would be realized.

It wasn't too long before utility companies and independent energy experts calculated that the actual CO_2 savings were miniscule (if any). That was due to the inherent nature of wind energy, and the realities of necessarily continuously balancing the grid, on a second by second basis, with fossil fuel generated electricity. The frequently cited Bentek study (How Less Became More) is a sample independent assessment of this aspect. More importantly, there has been zero scientific empirical proof provided by the wind industry to support their claims of consequential CO_2 reduction.

Suspecting that the CO_2 deception would soon be exposed, the wind lobbyists took pre-emptive action, and added another rationale to prop up their case: energy diversity. However, since our electricity system already had considerable diversity this hype never gained much traction. Back to the drawing board.

The next justification put forward by the wind marketers was energy independence. This cleverly played on the concern most people have about oil and Middle East instability. Many ads were promoting wind energy as a good way to reduce our dependence on Middle Eastern oil.

None of these ads mentioned that only about 1% of our electricity is generated from oil. Or that the U.S. exports more oil than we use for electricity. Or that our main import source for oil is Canada. Despite the significant omissions and misrepresentations, this claim still resonates with many people, so it continues to be pushed. Whatever works.

Knowing full well that the assertions used to date were specious, wind proponents manufactured still another claim: green jobs. This was carefully selected to coincide with widespread employment concerns.

Unfortunately, when independent qualified parties examined the situation more closely, they found that the claims were wildly exaggerated. Big surprise!

A very detailed critique of the jobs situation is at PTCFacts, Info. Listed there are TEN major reasons why using jobs as an argument is not appropriate or meaningful. Additionally there is a list of some 45 reports written by independent experts, and they all agree that renewable energy claims are based on numerous fallacies.

Relentlessly moving forward, wind marketers then tried the focus from jobs to economic development. The marketers typically utilized a computer program called JEDI to make bold projections. Unfortunately, JEDI is a totally inadequate model for accurately arriving at such numbers, for a variety of technical reasons. The economic development contentions have also been shown to be inaccurate, as they never take into account economic losses that result from wind energy implementation- for example agricultural losses due to bat killings, and job losses due to higher electricity costs for factories, hospitals, and numerous employers.

Along the way, yet another claim began making the rounds: that wind energy is low cost. This is surprisingly bold, considering that if that were really true, RES/RPS mandates would not be necessary. For some reason, all calculations showing wind to be low cost conveniently ignore exorbitant subsidies, augmentation costs, power adjusting, additional transmission costs, and so. Independent analyses of levelized costs (e.g. from the EIA) have concluded that when all applicable wind related costs are accurately calculated wind energy is MUCH more expensive than any conventional source we have. A subtle but significant difference between wind energy and other conventional sources of electricity is in power quality. This term refers to such technical performance factors as voltage transients, voltage variations, waveform distortion (e.g., harmonics), frequency variations, and so forth. The reality is that wind energy introduces many more of these issues than does a conventional power facility. Additional costs are needed to deal with these wind caused problems. These are rarely identified in pro-wind economic analyses.

When confronted with the reality that wind energy is considerably more expensive than any conventional source, a common rejoinder is to object to that by saying that once the "externalities" of conventional sources are taken into account, wind is less expensive than those conventional sources. To gullible sheeple, this might make sense. But consider the following two points. First, externality analyses posited by wind zealots never take into account the true environmental consequences of wind energy, rare earth impacts, human health effects, bird and bat deaths, and the CO_2 generated from a two million pound concrete base. Second, the externalities for things like coal are always only the negative part. If these advocates want a true big picture calculation, then they need to also add in the benefits to us from low cost coal based electricity. considering that coal played a major part in our economic success and improved health and living standards over the past century, such a plus factor would be enormous.

A key grid ingredient is Firm Capacity. A layman's translation is that this is an indication of dependability. Conventional sources like nuclear have a Firm Capacity of nearly 100%. Wind has a Firm Capacity of about 0%. Big difference! Since this enormous Firm Capacity discrepancy is indisputable, wind energy apologists then decided to adopt the strategy that wind energy isn't a "capacity resource" after all, but rather an "energy resource". Surprisingly, this may be the first contention that is actually true. But what does this really mean? The reality is that saying "wind is an energy source" is a trivial statement, on a par with saying lightning is an energy source.

One of the latest buzz words is "sustainability". The truth about "sustainability" is it is totally hypocritical to have wind advocates attacking fossil fuels as unsustainable, when the wind business has an ENORMOUS dependency on fossil fuels for their construction, delivery, maintenance, and operation. Wind energy is our least "sustainable option.

The claim that wind energy is "green" or "environmentally friendly" is laugh out loud hilarious. Consider just one part of a turbine, the generator, which uses considerable rare earth elements, 2000 pounds per KW. The mining and processing of these metals has horrific environmental consequences that are unacknowledged and ignored by the wind industry and its environmental surrogates. For instance, just the rare earths of a typical 100 MW wind project would generate approximately:

a. 20,000 square meters of destroyed vegetation.

b. 1.2 million pounds of CO_2.

c. 6 million cubic meters of toxic air pollution.

d. 29 million gallons of poisoned water.

e. 600 million pounds of highly contaminated tailing sands.

f. 280,000 pounds of radioactive waste.

Modern civilization is based on our ability to produce electrical POWER. Our modern sense of power is inextricably related to "controlled performance expectations": when we turn the knob, we expect the stove to go on 100% of the time -- not just on those wildly intermittent occasions when the wind is blowing within a certain speed range.

So, in effect, we have come around full circle. A hundred plus years ago, wind energy was recognized as antiquated, unreliable, and expensive source of energy -- and now, after hundreds of billions of wasted tax and consumer dollars, we find that (surprise) it still is an antiquated, unreliable, and expensive source of energy.

Here is an example of a community having problems with their wind turbines. Molly Line, a reporter for Fox News on February 26, 2013 wrote.

Cape Cod community considers taking down wind turbines after illness and noise. Two wind turbines towering above the Cape Cod community of Falmouth, Massachusetts were intended to produce green energy and savings -- but they created angst and division, and may now be removed at a high cost as neighbors complain of noise and illness.

"It gets to be jet -engine loud," said Falmouth resident Neil Andersen. He and his wife Betsy live just a quarter of mile from one of the turbines. They say the impact on their health has been devastating. They're suffering headaches, dizziness, and sleep deprivation and often seek to escape the property where they have lived for more than 20 years.

Every time the blade has a downward motion it gives off a tremendous energy, gives off a pulse," said

Andersen. "And that pulse, it gets into your tubular organs, chest cavity, mimics a heartbeat, gives you headaches. It's extremely disturbing and it gets to the point where you have to leave"

The first turbine went up in 2010 and by the time both were in place on the industrial site of the town's water treatment facility, the price was $10 million. Town officials say taking them down will cost an estimated $5 million to $15 million, but that is just what Falmouth's five selectmen have decided to move toward doing. "The selectmen unanimously voted to remove them. We think it's the right thing to do, absolutely, "Selectman David Brags said. "You can't put a monetary value on people's health and that's what's happened here. A lot of people are sick because of these."

The Obama administration gives wind farms a pass on eagle deaths, prosecutes oil companies. More than 573,000 birds are killed by the country's wind farms each year, including 83,000 hunting birds such as hawks, falcons, and eagles, according to an estimate published in March 2013 in the peer-reviewed Wildlife Society Bulletin.

Each death is a federal crime, a charge that the Obama administration has used to prosecute oil companies when birds drown in their waste pits, and power companies when birds are electrocuted by their power lines. No wind energy company has been prosecuted, even those that repeatedly flout the law.

Wind power is a cornerstone of President Barack Obama's energy plan. His administration has championed a $1 billion-a-year tax break.
Nearly all the birds being killed are protected under federal environmental laws, which prosecutors have used to generate tens of millions of dollars in fines and settlements from businesses, including oil and gas companies, over the past five years.

"What it boils down to is this: If you electrocute an eagle, that is bad, but if you chop it to pieces, that is

OK," said Tim Eicher, a former U.S. Fish and Wildlife Service enforcement agent based in Cody, Wyoming.

NATIONAL DEFENSE

As the first priority of the President and the Congress of the United States of America is NATIONAL DEFENSE then a look at today's, 2014, national defense and military is in order. America's main national defense relies on volunteers, as we have an all volunteer military force. The most trained of the military people are the active duty personnel. These are the backbone of our military defense. Besides the active duty personnel, we have the military reserves who are individuals who have left active duty. In order to utilize the reserves for combat duty the Commander in Chief needs to call them back to active duty. The reserves meet one weekend a month and two weeks a year for training. We also have the national guard that in essence are the state national guards. They meet like the reserves. In theory the state national guard units have as their primary mission to remain in their states to answer the call of any problem in their respective state. But the actual practice has recently been to have various state national guard units re-ploy to Iraq and Afghanistan for the war effort.

In 1960 when America had a population of 150 million people we had 2 million active duty military personnel. In 2014, America has a population of 315 million people and one million 400,000 on active duty. That's 600,000 less people on active duty but twice the population. Is this smart strategy? The world today is less safe than in 1960.

Today, our Army may be going to be reduced to 420,000 active duty military personnel. Our Marines are estimated to be around 175,000. The Air Force is estimated to be around 400,000. The Navy is estimated to be around 400,000. President Obama wants to reduce our active duty military personnel and our Congress goes along with whatever the President wants. Even though we have record tax revenues coming into the U.S. Treasury the politicians spend our money on other things and reduce our military budgets. A recent report that surfaced stated that the federal government reduced their manpower by ONE PERSON. For the record the military budget during President Eisenhower's years in office was 10% of the budget. Today's budget for the military is 4%. Are we smarter than a third grader?

FOR THE RECORD WE PUT 16.1 MILLION MEN AND WOMEN IN UNIFORM DURING WORLD WAR II. The record shows that 405,399 Americans were killed and 670,846 were wounded and 30,314 are still missing from World War II. That's over a million American people either killed or wounded. For the record, historians estimate that somewhere between 50 million to 70 million people worldwide were killed during World War II.

We weren't prepared for World War II, but we were even LESS prepared for the Korean War. After World War II we drastically downsized our military. The Chinese wanted Korea and they had almost complete control of what is now South Korea as we entered the war. We called up our reserves. The early months of fighting was brutal. Many Americans that went into battle had ONLY 2 weeks of military training. The military didn't even have enough ammunition. We had 36,516 Americans killed and 92,134 wounded.

The world today is a much faster and dangerous world. The weapons used today are many times more lethal. Missiles are held by almost every nation that has a military. The response time to build up a modern fighting military force if attacked will be minuscule compared to the attack on Pearl Harbor. The odds of rebounding from such an attack where we lost so many important naval pieces would be limited as many of those manufactures have either gone overseas or sold their plants to foreigners.

For example, during the 3 1/2 years of World War II that started with the Japanese bombing of Pearl Harbor in December 1941 and ended in August 1945, the United States PRODUCED; 22 aircraft carriers, 8 battleships, 48 cruisers, 349 destroyers, 203 submarines, 34 million tons of merchant ships, 100,000 fighter aircraft, 98,000 bombers, 24,000 transport aircraft, 58,000 training aircraft, 93,000 tanks, 257,000 artillery pieces, 105,000 mortars, 3,000,000 machine guns, and 2,500,000 military trucks.

If World War III broke out the odds of it lasting over 3 years with today's trigger happy nations who possess the latest technology would be a miracle. The odds are more inclined toward atomic bombs going off. Woe to the nation who cannot defend itself. Time will be of the essence and military preparedness will rule the day.

During President Ronald Reagan's years in office we had 15 aircraft carriers. Remember, President Jimmy Carter didn't believe in a strong military. He reduced our military capability. Today, we have 9 aircraft carriers and it has been reported that two will be retired leaving only 7. Just a reminder, there is more water in the world than land. Yes, the focus is more on airplanes, jet fighters, than ships or aircraft carriers. But we need more aircraft carriers because jet fighters can go anywhere in the world if they are ON an aircraft carrier. They launch from an aircraft carrier! It appears that President Obama is following in Carter's plan of reducing our military.

What we need now is a man like George Washington who did the impossible with the help from Divine intervention.

Retired Navy Commander Kirk Lippold, retired Air Force Lt. General Richard Newton, and retired Lt. General Jerry Boykin, said on the Mike Huckabee show on March 2, 2014, "that our military IS NOT able to carry out their missions." They further said, "our Allies are NOT sure if we will be there for them."

In a Senate Armed Services Committee hearing in April 2014 with Secretary of the Army John McHugh and Army Chief of Staff 4 Star General Raymond Odierno testifying, the following information is of note. General Odierno stated, "that we have a HIGH LEVEL OF RISK FOR THE ARMY FOR A CONTINUED CONFLICT LASTING MORE THAN A YEAR." The General further stated, "that to be ENGAGED IN TWO CONFLICTS IN DIFFERENT PARTS OF THE WORLD AT THE SAME TIME WOULD BE DIFFICULT." The Department of Defense has had cuts of $487 billion and then another cut of $500 billion which has created the present climate for the Army and the military. Further cuts to the DOD budget are scheduled for FY2016. Our military manpower is at pre-World War II levels. Both McHugh and Odierno agreed the world TODAY is a more dangerous place than any time since World War II.

Our Allies have also dramatically cut back on their militaries. It seems that the leadership of our Allies are in the same denial as the American leadership. Especially our European Allies who have a head start to socialism. It appears that the Europeans are worn out from the two world wars that were fought in their countries and the generations following the devastation are in self denial and have deceived themselves that peace comes from weakness. They seem to want peace at any cost. Their government leaders have embraced the idea that by giving their people what they want then all will be well. How foolish can people become! Every generation must fight the good fight to keep their freedoms. Socialism takes those freedoms away.

On CSPAN, U.S. 4 Star General Joseph Dunford, Afghanistan War Commander, at a congressional hearing said," 48 Americans were killed by Afghan trainees in 2013, and ONLY 14 so far in 2014." But that was on March 12, 2014! The way he said that it appeared he thought that was an improvement, but there are still 9 months left in 2014, and Americans role is primarily to train the Afghans. General Dunford was pushing for 10,000 Americans to stay in Afghanistan after 2014. President Obama had kept everyone in the dark about his decision on how many troops would remain in Afghanistan after 2014.

Dunford said, "the immediate deterioration of the Afghan military once we withdraw from Afghanistan in 2014 was his reason for the United States to remain there." He further said, "the plight of Afghan women would be dire if we withdrew." Dunford also said, "the Afghan air force is two years away from effectiveness."

He commented that most of the 31 major building projects that the United States either built or were working on have been blown up. That's hundreds of millions of dollars spent on nation building.

Whenever we leave Afghanistan it will likely follow the same course as Iraq which is close to civil war and controlled by militants who are not friendly to the United States. But on the other hand, NO nation in the history of Afghanistan has ever won or defeated the enemy there. Many nations have tried but none succeeded. The Russians tried for a decade and left without success. Should we continue to lose precious American lives in a country that eventually when we do leave will revert back into a disaster? Between Iraq and Afghanistan over 6200 Americans have been killed. Plus thousands more have been severely injured.

The results of another Congressional hearing committee, the House Intelligence Committee hearing with Mike Morrell in April 2014 revealed some shocking information. Mike Morrell was the Deputy Director of the CIA at the time of the September 11, 2012 Benghazi massacre. He also had experience as the Acting Director of the CIA. Morrell revealed that he depended on the CIA agents in Langley, Virginia and these CIA analysts DID NOT TALK TO ANYONE ON THE GROUND IN BENGHAZI. Morrell who has 33 years experience with the CIA said the event was caused by a video that produced a protest. The CIA station chief in Benghazi and numerous other CIA agents on the ground in Benghazi said it was a terrorist attack about 15 minutes after it started. Morrell said even after being informed by the people on the ground in Benghazi that he relied on the CIA analysts in Langley and he and they did not have to talk to anyone on the ground. What a startling revelation! How could anyone in a leadership role be so inefficient? So the question becomes WHY HAVE INTELLIGENCE OFFICERS ON THE GROUND IF THE LEADERSHIP DOESN'T LISTEN TO WHAT THEY HAVE TO SAY?

Morrell put the blame on the CIA analysts in Langley. But facts are stubborn things. The factual evidence has proven Morrell wrong. Within days after the attack EVEN Morrell claimed it was a terrorist attack. But the talking points by the Obama administration to the American public claimed it was a video that caused a protest. Susan Rice, who was the U.S. ambassador to the United Nations went on 5 Sunday television network shows to tell Americans that a video caused a protest. TWO WEEKS AFTER THE ATTACK, Barack Obama gave a speech to the United Nations claiming a video caused a protest. Think about this for a moment. How could a President of the United States of America go to the United Nations and give a speech that he knew was being broadcast all over the world and say it was the video that caused the massacre when anyone who was following the story knew it was a terrorist attack?

Mike Rogers, the Chairman of the House Intelligence Committee, said that he believed that Obama who had previously stated that Al Qaeda was on the run and therefore was incapable of doing any more harm. After all, the November 2012 presidential election was in just 6 weeks, and Obama wanted Americans to believe that he is a strong President. It appears that Mike Morrell's testimony was highly political to protect the State Department and Obama.

There were a number of warnings that an attack may happen in Benghazi. For several months prior to the attack several attacks had taken place throughout Benghazi. The British Embassy closed and left as well as the Red Cross. The Libyan government could not control the terrorists in Benghazi. Ambassador Stevens had pleaded to the State Department for help, and was repeatedly denied. So when the American Embassy was attacked in Benghazi no one should have been surprised. You be the judge, was and is it a COVER UP by Obama and Secretary of State Hillary Clinton?

Once an attack happens NO ONE KNOWS HOW LONG IT WILL LAST. The terrorist attack at

Benghazi lasted approximately 12 hours. The Department of Defense, Pentagon, claimed the State Department under Hillary Clinton had the final say if any help would go to rescue the Americans at Benghazi. No help was sent and four Americans were killed and others wounded. Knowing about the terrorist activities happening in Benghazi for months prior to the attack why weren't military assets placed nearby in case of any attack? Also, since NO ONE KNEW WHEN THE ATTACK WOULD END WHY DIDN'T THE OBAMA ADMINISTRATION SEND HELP? The above information about the Benghazi event came from Catherine Herridage, who is one of the most trusted reporters in the business.

Benghazi was and still is a major problem today. But the bigger problem in the United States of America today is the lack of leadership. How is it that a few INEFFECTIVE POLITICIANS CAN CAUSE THE UNITED STATES OF AMERICA TO BE LED IN SUCH A NEGATIVE WAY. More and more Americans believe that President Barack Obama is leading us in the wrong direction. More and more Americans believe that Harry Reid, the Senate Majority Leader, is incapable of leading the Senate, is Obama's pawn and is helping to lead our once great nation into being a third world country. And, more and more Americans believe that Speaker of the House John Boehner has allowed himself to become Obama's pawn as his actions demonstrate a closer relationship with him than with the conservatives of his own political party. Boehner alone could have stopped some of the negative bills from becoming laws. Power is in the hands of these three men. These three men will be FOREVER LINKED TOGETHER AS WHAT THEY ARE. OBAMA, REID AND BOEHNER THE NAMES THAT WILL LIVE IN INFAMY. LIFE ON THIS EARTH IS SHORT COMPARED TO ETERNITY AS THEY WILL FIND OUT ON JUDGMENT DAY.

The United States of America according to our Constitution is a democratic republic. At least that is the theory, but in actual practice the three people mentioned above, Obama, Reid, and Boehner dictate through their massive power what the 315 million Americans must live with and under. The Constitution spells out that politicians "serve" the people. That means they "work" for the people. Most Americans want less federal government in their daily lives. But we are now heading for a dismantling of our rights as the Progressive Democratic Party is leading us closer and closer to socialism. Under socialism the individual's rights are controlled by the federal government. History has proven that socialism does NOT work. Socialism leads to tyranny.

Most Americans don't think of America as an empire. But other countries may perceive us in that light. No matter if we do or not America is judged by historians as an empire as we are compared to the great empires of history. The great empires of history are HISTORY. Why? For the most empires in the last 2000 years it was because their politicians, "leaders", gave the people more entitlements than they could afford bankrupting them. Social programs kept the politicians in power as the people kept them in because the people always wanted more. Once a government starts giving to people who don't work or who haven't worked for the entitlement than INCENTIVE to work is lost. As more people see others taking advantage of the entitlement society they feel that they too should receive them. After all the government is giving out free money with no strings attached. More than half of the American people are receiving entitlements, many who have not earned them. Is the fate of the United States of America the same as the empires that are now HISTORY? We now spend our money on social programs instead of our national defense. Are we at a point of no return? Is it just a matter of time? Not if, but when? Can we ever take away what has been given? And can we do it without civil unrest?

It seems that the Obama administration and supported by our Congress are spending more for social programs. But the first priority of any President and Congress is to have a strong national defense, a strong military. President Obama and our Congress are downsizing our active duty military to pre-World War II levels.

The world today is less safe than in 1960. China, that's Communist China, began a modernization of all of their military weapons systems over 15 years ago. They have been building up all of their military educational programs, military computer systems, offensive and defensive military capability, and leadership training. They have recently completed building a state of the art aircraft carrier to go along with their recent improvements for the navy. Their air force is becoming more modernized and will soon rival America's capabilities.

China's CYBER ESPIONAGE operation yielded sensitive technology and aircraft secrets from the United States which it was able to use in building its new J-20 stealth fighter jet. This was reported by Joe Battaglia on March 13, 2014. For example, the Washington Free Beacon reported, that nearly two dozen of America's major weapons systems were stolen, including the Joint Strike fighter, also known as the F-35 Lightning II, the most technically challenging weapons program the Pentagon has ever attempted. The Wall Street Journal also reported on this. The Chinese stealth fighter flew on March 1, 2014. The Chinese not only have many of our valuable designs, but they know how to build them. Richard Fisher, a Chinese weapon systems specialist with the International Assessment and Strategy Center, said the new J-20 demonstrated the enhanced fifth-generation jet fighter features. Representative Michael McCaul, Chairman of the House Homeland Security Subcommittee on Oversight, Investigations and Management, warned that cyber attacks, such as the one executed by the Chinese, place the country at risk.

Top media outlets in China recently boasted of the country's "awesome" nuclear capability. They released detailed strike plans. If enacted, the attacks could claim 50 million American lives. The report revealed that China is capable of striking major cities on the west coast via submarine launch. Their land based launch systems put New York, Philadelphia, and Annapolis within their range. Such an attack would cripple the west coast of the U.S., claiming 12 million lives in the INITIAL strike. People as far inland as Chicago would be affected by the resulting radiation. East coast strikes could claim up to an eighth of our population.

China's active duty army has 2 million well trained and well equipped personnel. China has millions in their reserve units. The population of China is 1.3 BILLION people, four times as many as the United States. The Bible mentions a war that one nation has an army of 200 million people, no other country could have this many except China.

America has fought in two wars against China, in Korea and Vietnam. Korea became a stalemate. Vietnam became at best a stalemate. When the war ended the North Vietnamese backed by China took over the U.S. backed South Vietnamese and millions of South Vietnamese were killed. America lost 58,209 men and women!

This author is amazed when retired American generals spout off on television about how weak China's military is. These generals seem to underestimate China's military effectiveness and capability.

And these retired American generals claim that Russia is weak. Russia, too, has been building up its military capability under their leader, Vladimir Putin. In September 2013, Russia launched large scale war exercises that included use of several nuclear capable missiles. Their military may not rival America's, but they have enough missiles to do a great deal of harm.

North Korea has an active duty army of one million people.

Pakistan has about 190 million people. Their military weapons include approximately 100 nuclear weapons. Pakistan doesn't like us.

Iran, Hezbollah, and Hamas don't like us.

Al Queda and all of their terrorists cells all over the world don't like us.

Our two major European Allies, Great Britain and France, combined have LESS than 150,000 active duty military personnel.

Two of our other major Allies, Germany and Japan, don't have militaries. After World War II they were forbidden to have a military. They do have a peace keeping force.

If it came to an all out war, would it be America with some help from Great Britain, France, Canada, Australia, and Israel AGAINST China, Russia, North Korea, Iran, Pakistan, Syria, Venezuela, and Al-

Queda? It is important to note the Bible that it is written that the end times, the world will be destroyed by fire this time presumably from nuclear weapons. If America is weak or presumed to be weak than a war is more likely to occur. But if we are strong or presumed to be than the odds decrease of any attack. Our army is the same size as before World War II, our navy's number of military ships are the same size as 1917, and our air force's fighter aircraft is almost the size as of 1945. Plus, our air force depends on refueling tankers built in the 1960s. Our manufacturing capability of weapons systems is at an all time low as much of our manufacturing plants are in China.

HOW SAFE DO YOU FEEL NOW? IS THIS A GOOD TIME TO DOWNSIZE OUR MILITARY?

As President Obama is downsizing our military, he is making America more dependent on computers which is mostly dependent on our nation's electric grid. It may be analyzed that Obama relies on technology and computers more than on human manpower. BUT, what if the technology and computers are compromised or inoperative? The fight for computer security has become an almost impossible endeavor. Countries are now "hacking" into each others computer systems with regularity. A virus can be planted into almost any computer system This may make the computer system unreliable.

One important thing to keep in mind is that computers rely on a power supply. That power supply is either a battery or a power outlet. The power outlet is connected to an electrical grid. An electrical grid is an interconnected network for delivering electricity from suppliers to consumers. It consists of generating stations that produce electric power, high voltage transmission lines that carry power from distant sources to demand centers, and distribution lines that connect individual customers.

The electrical grid's power delivery infrastructures suffer aging across the developed world.

Contributing factors to the current state of the electric grid and its consequences include:

1. Aging power equipment -- older equipment have higher failure rates, leading to customer interruption rates affecting the economy and society; also, older assets and facilities lead to higher inspection maintenance costs and further repair/restoration costs.

2. Obsolete system layout -- older areas require serious additional substation sites and rights-of-way that cannot be obtained in current area and are forced to use existing, insufficient facilities.

3. Outdated engineering -- traditional tools for power delivery planning and engineering are ineffective in addressing current problems of aged equipment, obsolete system layouts, and modern deregulated loading levels.

4. Old cultural value -- planning, engineering, operating of system using concepts and procedures that worked in vertically integrated industry exacerbate the problem under a deregulated industry.

An additional problem which may be far worse than those of the aging infrastructure has developed. On April 16, 2013 an attack on an electric substation occurred near San Jose, California, that nearly knocked out Silicon Valley's power supply.

Representative Henry Waxman, a Democratic Congressman from California, described the attack as, "an unprecedented and sophisticated attack on an electric grid substation with military style weapons. Communications were disrupted. The attack inflicted substantial damage."

Jon Wellinghoff, Chairman of the Federal Energy Regulatory Commission at the time, called it, "the most significant incident of domestic terrorism involving the U.S. power grid that has ever occurred."

It was further reported that if an enemy found the RIGHT NINE POWER SUBSTATIONS they could halt the nation's electric power grid system.

If an enemy knocked out our electric power grid everything would be at a standstill. Even most of our military which depends heavily on the electric power grid with many weapons systems depending on computers would be at a great disadvantage. So, does anyone see any problem with being so heavily dependent on our electric power grid? Think for a moment about how we use power in this country.

So what is our foreign policy? Can we describe our foreign policy as an "appeasement policy"? President Obama wants to negotiate everything with every foreign country to the point where the United States is giving away far more than what we are getting in return. But for some reason Obama rarely negotiates with the U.S. Congress. Several examples of Obama's negotiation skills were:

1. The START TREATY was very much a one sided negotiation in favor of Russia. The author's experience as one of America's original international inspectors during the First International Disarmament event in 1968 provides experience in this field. Also,

101

the author's experiences as a management consultant to over 300 corporations including many labor-management negotiations as the chief negotiator. Anyone interested in more details about this topic is available in one of the author's previous books. Remember, who led the fight to ratify the START TREATY in the Senate? Senator John Kerry!

2. Now, Kerry is our Secretary of State. With Kerry negotiating on behalf of the USA we all should be worried as he has a tendency to make a bad deal. Remember, Syria? As of this writing, Syria has NOT destroyed ALL of their chemical weapons.

3. Remember, Iraq? Under Obama's leadership, Secretary of State Hillary Clinton couldn't make a deal with Iraq, resulting in Iraq falling back into a chaotic killing field. All that American blood and treasure lost.

4. Afghanistan. Under Secretary Clinton and Secretary Kerry, Afghanistan has become a more dangerous place. After all of our military troops leave Afghanistan it appears that they will follow into the same chaos as Iraq.

President Obama's "appeasement policy" to the world goes back to his attitude expressed in his Cairo, Egypt speech where he stated that the United States of America was responsible for many of the problems of the world. He apologized to the world on behalf of America.

Other foreign policy mistakes were Benghazi where our ambassador and 3 others were assassinated by terrorists on September 11, 2012. After many warnings of terrorist activity in the region our President and Secretary of State Hillary Clinton dropped the ball by not having our American people leave this volatile area especially after other western nations left.

Also, SEQUESTER was the fault of President Obama, the Democrats and Republicans. While SEQUESTER had a major negative impact on our military it had limited impact on our federal government. It appears that our foreign aid to the world did not suffer. Our Washington elite politicians think that they can spend our American tax dollars at will. Over the last several years they have provided direct cash aid to:

1. Hamas -- $351 million

2. Libya -- $1.45 billion

3. Egypt -- $397 million

4. Mexico -- $622 million

5. Russia -- $380 million

6. Haiti -- $1.4 billion

7. Jordan -- $463 million

8. Kenya -- $816 million

9. Sudan -- $870 million

10. Nigeria -- $456 million

11. Uganda -- $451 million

12. Congo -- $359 million

13. Ethiopia -- $981 million

14. Pakistan -- $2 billion

15. South Africa -- $566 million

16. Senegal -- $698 million

17. Mozambique -- $404 million

18. Zambia -- $331 million

19. Kazakhstan -- $304 million

20. Iraq -- $1.08 billion

21. Tanzania -- $554 million

Our Washington politicians say America is broke! You can see why! But these Washington politicians can't help our VETERANS, SENIORS, AND HOMELESS.

But there is more! Our politicians also give a TON of money to the United Nations. How much? How much money does the United States currently contribute to the United Nations and its various agencies? No one knows for sure!

The State Department asked for $1.57 BILLION to give to international agencies in its 2014 State budget including $617.6 million for the UN operating budget. Other U.S. agencies giving to the UN include the DEPARTMENTS of Labor, Energy, Agriculture, Defense, and Health and Human Services.

Senator Mike Enzi of Wyoming said in a statement, "It's disturbing that no one, including our ambassador to the United Nations, knows exactly how much money we send the U.N. every year."

The last OMB (Office of Management and Budget) report to Congress on U.N. contributions was issued in June 2011 and covered fiscal 2010. It showed that the State Department was just one of 17 government agencies giving money to U.N. organizations, funds, affiliates, and other bodies, and the total expenditure that year was $7.69 BILLION.

The above information was reported by CNS News.

There have been reports that Obama is in favor of a "one world government" under the authority of the United Nations. That would destroy our sovereignty. DOUGLAS CASE, A CLASSMATE OF BILL CLINTON AT GEORGETOWN UNIVERSITY, SAID, "FOREIGN AID MIGHT BE DEFINED AS A TRANSFER OF MONEY FROM POOR PEOPLE IN RICH COUNTRIES TO RICH PEOPLE IN POOR COUNTRIES."

President John F. Kennedy held a dinner in the White House for a group of the brightest minds in the nation at that time. He made this statement: "This is perhaps the assembly of the most intelligence ever to gather at one time in the White House with the exception of when Thomas Jefferson dined alone."

Author's note the Founding Fathers never dined in the White House as a group. They were the most intelligent, wisest men ever to assemble anywhere.

Here are some of Thomas Jefferson's quotes:

"The democracy will cease to exist when you take away from those who are willing to work and give to those who would not."

"When we get piled upon one another in large cities, as in Europe, we shall become as corrupt as Europe."

"It is incumbent on every generation to pay its own debts as it goes. A principle which if acted on would save one-half the wars of the world."

"I predict future happiness for Americans if they can prevent the government from wasting the labors of the people under the pretense of taking care of them."

"My reading of history convinces me that most bad government results from too much government."

"No free man shall ever be debarred the use of arms."

"The strongest reason for the people to retain the right to keep and bear arms is, as a last resort, to protect themselves against tyranny in government."

"The tree of liberty must be refreshed from time to time with the blood of patriots and tyrants."

"To compel a man to subsidize with his takes the propagation of ideas which he disbelieves is sinful and tyrannical."

"A government big enough to give you everything you want, is strong enough to take everything you have."

"All tyranny needs to gain a foothold is for people of good conscience to remain silent."

Here are several quotes from some other people:

President Ronald Reagan said, "Government's view of the economy could be summed up in a few short phrases: If it moves, tax it. If it keeps moving, regulate it. And if it stops moving, subsidize it."

Winston Churchill said, "The inherent vice of capitalism is the unequal sharing of the blessings. The inherent blessing of socialism is the equal sharing of misery."

President James Madison said, "A well instructed people alone can be permanently a free people."

President James Madison said, "We have staked the whole future of American civilization, not on the power of government, far from it. We've staked the future of all our political institutions upon our capacity to sustain ourselves according to the Ten Commandments of God."

The Tenth Amendment to the Constitution of the United States of America.

The powers not delegated to the United States by the Constitution, nor prohibited by it to the States, are reserved to the States respectively, or to the people.

The Constitution is clear, but why has the federal government assumed some of the rights expressly reserved for the states?

DO WE NEED A VOTER ID?

1. In 59 voting districts in the Philadelphia region, Obama received 100% of the votes with not even a single vote recorded for Romney.

2. In 21 districts in Wood County, Ohio, Obama received 100% of the votes where GOP inspectors were illegally removed from their polling locations -- and not one single vote was recorded for Romney.

3. In Wood County, Ohio, 106,258 voted in a county with only 98,213 eligible voters.

4. In St. Lucie County, Florida, there were 175,574 registered eligible voters, but 247,713 votes were cast.

5. The National Seal Museum, a polling location in St. Lucie County, Florida, had a 158% voter turnout.

6. Palm Beach County, Florida had a 141% voter turnout.

7. In one Ohio county, Obama won by 108% of the total number of eligible voters.

8. According to the Virginia Voters Alliance, 44,000 people are registered to vote in both Maryland and Virginia. They also found 31,000 dead voters through the Social Security Administration's Death Master File. The president of the organization said that dead voter registration is a prime target for voter fraud.

9. NOTE -- Obama won in every state that did NOT require a photo ID and lost in every state that did require a photo ID in order to vote.

Voting is one of the most sacred and basic rights of American citizens. To not require a voter to present an ID card is beyond fantasy. In just an hour this author thought of 38 activities that require an ID card. There is no acceptable reason that an American citizen does not have an ID card. The following list requires an ID card and there are more activities that may require the use of an ID card.

1. opening a bank checking account

2. opening a bank savings account

3. cashing a check

4. stopped by police / law enforcement

5. obtain a passport or visa

6. purchase auto / or truck license plates

7. applying for a driver's license

8. renewing a driver's license

9. to board Amtrak

10. to register for college

11. to take SAT test

12. to take ACT test

13. to pick up a child at grade school entrance if other than a parent

14. purchase vehicle insurance

15. to purchase handicap placard

16. to purchase beer / alcohol

17. entrance to hospital ER

18. entrance to government buildings

19. to purchase cigarettes

20 .to get a fishing license

21. to purchase a handgun / rifle

22. to use a credit card

23. to apply for a government job

24. to apply for a teaching job

25. to apply for most jobs during interview / acceptance of job

26. airport check in for flight ticket

27. to go through airport customs

28. to go through airport pat down if buzzer goes off

29. winning a contest or lottery

30. turning in Dish equipment

31. to register to vote

32. to vote

33. to register for hotel or motel

34. to open escrow to buy a house

35. to get food stamps

36. to get welfare payments

37. to get disability insurance payments

38. The Democratic Party required their delegates to show their ID card to enter their convention. They want to know who is in their building but not who is voting. Does that make any sense?

For any political party NOT TO want a person to show an ID card one must question his/her motive.

There was also a question about computer fraud. It appears that a number of people complained that they voted for Romney but on the last frame of their ballot the computer changed their vote to Obama. The voting machines can be programmed to whatever the programmer is paid to do. Did the computer malfunction or was the computer software rigged? We may never know the answer. The Department of Justice under Eric Holder would have the responsibility to investigate the problem. That could be like the fox guarding the hen house.

The ONLY fair and honest way to have accurate results would be to have PAPER BALLOTS for both political parties to look at. A law should be passed that the PAPER BALLOTS shall be kept for a year.

DECEPTION!
A Story of Deception by Kitty Werthmann

What I am about to tell you is something you're probably never heard or will ever read in history books.

I believe that I am an eyewitness to history. I cannot tell you that Hitler took Austria by tanks and guns; it would distort history. We elected him by a landslide — 98% of the vote. I've never read that in any American publications.

Everyone thinks that Hitler just rolled in with tanks and took Austria by force.

In 1938, Austria was in deep depression. Nearly one-third of our workforce was unemployed. We had 25% inflation and 25% bank loan interest rates.

Farmers and business people were declaring bankruptcy daily. Young people were going from house to house begging for food. Not that they didn't want to work; there simply weren't any jobs. My mother was a Christian woman and believed in helping people in need. Every day we cooked a big kettle of soup and baked bread to feed the poor, hungry people -- about 30 daily.

The Communist Party and the National Socialist Party were fighting each other. Blocks and blocks of cities like Vienna, Linz, and Graz were destroyed. The people became desperate and petitioned the government to let them decide what kind of government they wanted.

We looked to our neighbor on the north, Germany, where Hitler had been in power since 1933. We had been told that they didn't have unemployment or crime, and they had a high standard of living. Nothing was ever said about persecution of any group -- Jewish or otherwise. We were led to believe that everyone was happy. We wanted the same way of life in Austria. We were promised that a vote for Hitler would mean the end of unemployment and help for the family. Hitler also said that businesses would be assisted, and farmers would get their farms back. Ninety-eight percent of the population voted to annex Austria to Germany and have Hitler for our ruler.

We were overjoyed, and for three days we danced in the streets and had candlelight parades. The new government opened up big field kitchens and everyone was fed.

After the election, German officials were appointed, and like a miracle, we suddenly had law and order. Three or four weeks later, everyone was employed. The government made that a lot of work was created through the Public Work Service.

Hitler decided we should have equal rights for women. Before this, it was a custom that married

Austrian women did not work outside the home. An able-bodied husband would be looked down on if he couldn't support his family. Many women in the teaching profession were elated that they could retain the jobs they previously had been required to give up for marriage.

Hitler Targets Education -- Eliminates Religious Instruction for Children:

Our education was nationalized. I attended a very good public school. The population was predominantly Catholic, so we had religion in our schools. The day we elected Hitler (March 13, 1938), I walked into my schoolroom to find the crucifix replaced by Hitler's picture hanging next to a Nazi flag. Our teacher, a very devout woman, stood up and told the class we wouldn't pray or have religion anymore. Instead, we sang "Deutschland, Deutschland, Uber Alles", and had physical education.

Sunday became National Youth Day with compulsory attendance. Parents were not pleased about the sudden change in curriculum. They were told that if they did not send us, they would receive a stiff letter of warning the first time. The second time they would be fined the equivalent of $300, and the third time they would be subject to jail. The first two hours consisted of political indoctrination. The rest of the day we had sports. As time went along, we loved it. Oh, we had so much fun and got our sports equipment free. We would go home and gleefully tell our parents about the wonderful time we had.

My mother was very unhappy. When the next term started, she took me out of public school and put me in a convent. I told her she couldn't do that and she told me that someday when I grew up, I would be grateful. There was a very good curriculum, but hardly any fun -- no sports, and no political indoctrination. I hated it at first but felt I could tolerate it. Every once in a while, on holidays, I went home. I would go back to my old friends and ask what was going on and what they were doing. Their loose lifestyle was very alarming to me. They lived without religion. By that time unwed mothers were glorified for having a baby for Hitler. It seemed strange to me that our society changed so suddenly. As time went along, I realized what a great deed my mother did so I wasn't exposed to that kind of humanistic philosophy.

Equal Rights Hits Home:

In 1939, the war started and a food bank was established. All food was rationed and could only be purchased using food stamps. At the same time, a full employment law was passed which meant if you didn't work, you didn't get a ration card, and if you didn't have a card, you starved to death. Women who stayed home to raise their families didn't have any marketable skills and often had to take jobs more suited for men.

Soon, after this, the draft was implemented. It was compulsory for young people, male and female, to give one year to the labor corps. During the day, the girls worked on the farms, and at night they returned to their barracks for military training just like the boys. They were trained to be anti-aircraft gunners and participated in the signal corps. After the labor corps, they were not discharged but were used in the front lines. When I go back to Austria to visit my family and friends, most of these women are emotional cripples because they just were not equipped to handle the horrors of combat.

Three months before I turned 18, I was severely injured in an air raid attack. I nearly had a leg amputated, so I was spared having to go into the labor corps and into military service.

Hitler Restructured the Family Through Daycare:
When the mothers had to go into the work force, the government immediately established child care centers. You could take your children ages 4 weeks to school age and leave them there around the clock, 7 days a week, under the total care of the government.

The state raised a whole generation of children. There were no motherly women to take care of the children, just people highly trained in child psychology. By this time, no one talked about equal rights. We knew we had been had.

Health Care and Small Business Suffer Under Government Controls:

Before Hitler, we had very good medical care. Many American doctors trained at the University of Vienna. After Hitler, health care was socialized, free for everyone. Doctors were salaried by the government. The problem was, since it was free, the people were going to the doctors for everything. When the good doctor arrived at his office at 8 a.m., 40 people were already waiting and, at the same time, the hospitals were full. If you needed elective surgery, you had to wait a year or two for your turn. There was no money for research as it was poured into socialized medicine. Research at the medical schools literally stopped, so the best doctors left Austria and emigrated to other countries.

As for healthcare, our tax rates went up to 80% of our income. Newlyweds immediately received a $1,000 loan from the government to establish a household. We had big programs for families. All day care and education were free. High Schools were taken over by the government and college tuition was subsidized. Everyone was entitled to free handouts, such as food stamps, clothing, and housing.

We had another agency designed to monitor business. My brother-in-law owned a restaurant that had square tables. Government officials told him he had to replace them with round tables because people might bump themselves on the corners. Then they said he had to have additional bathroom facilities. It was just a small dairy business with a snack bar. He couldn't meet all the demands. Soon, he went out of business. If the government owned the large businesses and not many small ones existed, it could be in control.

We had consumer protection. We were told how to shop and what to buy. Free enterprise was essentially abolished. We had a planning agency specially designed for farmers. The agents would go to the farms, count the live-stock, then tell the farmers what to produce, and how to produce it.

"Mercy Killing" Redefined:

In 1944, I was a student teacher in a small village in the Alps. The villagers were surrounded by mountain passes which, in the winter, were closed off with snow, causing people to be isolated. so people intermarried and offspring were sometimes retarded. When I arrived, I was told there were 15 mentally retarded adults, but they were all useful and did good manual work. I knew one, named Vincent, very well. He was a janitor of the school. One day I looked out the window and saw Vincent and others getting into a van. I asked my superior where they were going. She said to an institution where the State Health Department would teach them a trade, and to read and write. The families were required to sign papers with a little clause that they could not visit for 6 months. They were told visits would interfere with the program and might cause homesickness.

As time passed, letters started to dribble back saying these people died a natural merciful death. The villagers were not fooled. We suspected what was happening. Those people left in excellent physical health and all died within 6 months. We called this euthanasia.

The Final Steps -- Gun Laws:

Next came gun registration. People were getting injured by guns. Hitler said that the real way to catch criminals (we still had a few) was by matching serial numbers on guns. Most citizens were law abiding and dutifully marched to the police station to register their firearms. Not long after-wards, the police said it was best for everyone to turn in their guns. The authorities already knew who had them, so it was futile not to comply voluntarily.

No more freedom of speech. Anyone who said something against the government was taken away. We knew many people who were arrested not only Jews, but also priests and ministers who spoke up.

Totalitarianism didn't come quickly, it took 5 years from 1938 to 1943, to realize full dictatorship in Austria. Had it happened overnight, my countrymen would have fought to the last breath. Instead, we had creeping gradualism.

Now our only weapons were broom handles. The whole idea sounds almost unbelievable that the state, little by little eroded our freedom.

After World War II, Russian troops occupied Austria. Women were raped, preteen to elderly. The press never wrote about this either. When the Soviets left in 1955, they took everything that they could, dismantling whole factories in the process. They sawed down whole orchards of fruit, and what they couldn't destroy, they burned. We called it The

Burned Earth. Most of the population barricaded themselves in their houses. Women hid in their cellars for 6 weeks as the troops mobilized. Those who couldn't, paid the price. There is a monument in Vienna today, dedicated to those women who were massacred by the Russians. This is an eye witness account.

It's true-- those of us who sailed past the Statue of Liberty came to a country of unbelievable freedom and opportunity.

America Truly is the Greatest Country in the World. Don't Let Freedom Slip Away, AFTER AMERICA, THERE IS NO PLACE TO GO.

This was written by Kitty Werthmann, Word for word.

When things get tough it is easy to be deceived. What happened to the people of Austria is what deception looks like. Is the United States of America following in the same footsteps, gradually step by step?

A FATHER-DAUGHTER TALK:

A young woman was about to finish her first year of college. Like so many others her age, she considered herself to be very liberal, and among other liberal ideals, was very much in favor of higher taxes to support more government programs, in other words redistribution of wealth. She was deeply ashamed that her father was a staunch conservative, a feeling she openly expressed. Based on the lectures that she had participated in, and the occasional chat with a professor, she felt that her father had for years harbored an evil, selfish desire to keep what he thought should be his.

One day she was challenging her father on his opposition to higher taxes on the rich and the need for more government programs.

The self-professed objectivity proclaimed by her professors had to be the truth and she indicated so to her father. He responded by asking how she was doing in school. Taken aback, she answered rather haughtily that she had a 4.0 GPA, and let him know that it was tough to maintain, insisting that she was taking a very difficult course load and was constantly studying, which left her no time to go out and party like other people she knew. She didn't even have time for a boyfriend, and didn't really have many college friends because she spent all her time studying.

Her father listened and then asked, "How is your friend Audrey doing?"

She replied, "Audrey is barely getting by. All she takes are easy classes, she never studies, and she barely has a 2.0 GPA. She is so popular on campus: college for her is a blast. She's always invited to all the parties and lots of times she doesn't even show up for classes because she's too hung over."

Her wise father asked his daughter, "Why don't you go to the Dean's office ask him to deduct 1.0 off your

GPA and give it to your friend who only has a 2.0. That way you will both have a 3.0 GPA and certainly that would be fair and equal distribution of GPA."

The daughter, visibly shocked by her father's suggestion, angrily fired back, "That's a crazy idea, how would that be fair! I've worked really hard for my grades! I've invested a lot of time, and a lot of hard work! Audrey has done next to nothing toward her degree. She played while I worked my tail off!"

The father slowly smiled, winked and said gently, "Welcome to the conservative side of the fence."

HOW TO CREATE A SOCIAL STATE, SOCIALISM

By Saul Alinsky

There are 8 levels of CONTROL before you are able to create a social state.

1. Healthcare -- Control healthcare and you control the people.

2. Poverty -- Increase the POVERTY level as high as possible, poor people are easier to CONTROL and will not fight back if you are providing everything for them to live.

3. Debt -- Increase the debt to an unsustainable level. That way you are able to increase taxes, and this will produce more poverty.

4. Gun Control -- Remove the ability to defend themselves from the government. That way you are able to create a police state.

5. Welfare -- Take CONTROL of every aspect of their lives -- food, housing and income.

6. Education -- Take CONTROL of what people read and listen to -- take CONTROL of what children learn in school.

7. Religion -- Remove the belief in God from government and schools.

8. Class Warfare -- Divide the people into the wealthy and the poor. This will cause more discontent and it will be easier to take (tax) the wealthy with the support of the poor.

Question -- Does any of this sound like what is happening to the United States?

We Americans want whoever is elected to be our President to be successful in solving our nation's problems according to the United States Constitution and the Rule of Law(s). As this book is about facts, it is with sadness that a list of problems or scandals have occurred during President Obama's time in office.

Here are some of the problems or scandals that we know about:

1. IRS targets Obama's enemies, the conservative groups.

2. Benghazi -- the failure to remove or protect the people in the embassy and the talking points that a video caused the attack

3. The Justice Department watching the Associated Press reporters phone records as part of a leak investigation.

4. The Justice Department monitoring James Rosen's phone and emails.

5. The ATF Fast and Furious program. Allowed weapons from the U.S. to "walk" across the border into the hands of Mexican drug dealers.

6. HHS Secretary Kathleen Sebelius solicited donations from companies HHS might regulate.

7. The Pigford scandal. Agriculture Department effort that started as an attempt to compensate black

farmers who had been discriminated against by the agency but evolved into a gravy train delivering several billion dollars in cash to thousands of additional minority and female farmers who probably didn't face discrimination.

8. The GSA, General Services Administration, in 2010 held an $823,000 training conference in Las Vegas.

9. Veterans Affairs in Disney World. The agency spent more than $6 million on two conferences in Orlando, Florida.

10. Sebelius violates the Hatch Act. A U.S. special counsel determined that Sebelius violated the Hatch Act when she made "extemporaneous partisan remarks" during a speech in her official capacity.

11. Solyndra

12. The Justice Department was accused of using a racial double standard in failing to pursue a voter intimidation case against Black Panthers who appeared to be menacing voters at a polling place in 2008 in Philadelphia.

13. Obama may have violated the Constitution and both the letter and spirit of the War Powers Resolution by attacking Libya without congressional approval.

14. President Obama has repeatedly been accused of making end runs around Congress by deciding which laws to enforce, including the decision not to deport illegal immigrants who may have been allowed to stay in the United States had Congress passed the "Dream Act."

15. The sudden decision to arrest Nakoula Basseley Nakoula on unrelated charges after protests in the Arab world over his anti-Muslim video.

16. The VA health care scandal.

17. The POW swap of Sgt Bergdahl for 5 GITMO detainees all who were at risk people to return to the battlefield.

America is a nation built on the RULE OF LAW(S). When a President and his administration doesn't enforce the RULE OF LAW, our nation is in danger. The United States of America was established with three separate branches of government, the executive, the legislative, and the judicial. Each branch was given equal powers. The theory has worked fairly well. But NOW we as a nation are vulnerable as never before as the legislative branch has broken down as the U.S. Senate controlled by Senator Harry Reid has become a pawn of the executive branch. The Constitution states that it's the Congress that makes the laws and then signed by a President. But when the members of Congress allow themselves to be controlled by their political party or by their President than we have a dangerous power grab that is potentially injurists to our Constitution and the American people. Harry Reid wouldn't be able to do his power grab IF the Democratic Party leaders in the Senate weren't supporting him. The two Senate Democratic Party leaders with unusual power are Senator Dick Durbin who originally introduced Obama in 2004 at the Democratic National Convention and Senator Chuck Shummer.

There have been a number of reports that bills to be considered by our Senators and Representatives that MANY IF NOT MOST DON'T EVEN READ THE BILLS! These bills become law and have surprises in them that only come to light after a period of time and usually after causing irrecoverable harm. A good example of this was the Affordable Care Act, more commonly known as Obamacare. We pay our Senators and Representatives a lot of money to do the job they were elected for. Each receives at least $174,000 a year plus other benefits. AND THEY CAN'T EVEN READ THE BILLS BEFORE VOTING ON THEM! There are no words to describe how disgraceful this is. No wonder our country is in such a big mess!

Do you remember the 2012 Democratic National Convention? The heart and soul of the delegates to that convention was at stake as they DID NOT WANT TO INCLUDE GOD IN THEIR PLATFORM. Remember? Twice they voted against having God in their platform. But then a hero emerged. It was

Antonio Villaraigosa, the Mayor of Los Angeles, who called for a third vote. It appeared the delegates still didn't approve of putting God in, but Villaraigosa declared the vote passed and God was in the platform despite most of the delegates didn't want any mention of religion. The Mayor who is a Hispanic realized to get the Hispanic vote religion had to be mentioned in the party's platform.

The problems that we have nationally are not only a fiscal one but a moral and cultural one. Dozens of nations have been bankrupted and rebounded. NO NATION HAS EVER RECOVERED FROM MORAL AND CULTURAL COLLAPSE.

Can your political party save you from going to HELL? POLITICIANS ARE NOT EXEMPT FROM GOING TO HELL! Can the Democratic Party or the Progressive Party or the Socialist Party SAVE you from going to HELL? NO!

It appears that the Democratic Party is MORE progressive or socialist than what the original Democratic Party used to be. Can the Republican Party or Libertarian Party SAVE you from going to HELL? NO! Then why do our U.S. Senators and U.S. Representatives DENY God in their speeches and votes? Yes, there may be a few who don't, but listen to them and follow their votes. They for the most part put their political party ahead of God and country. Many, if not most vote for their own gain. The weak among them can't put two sentences together without demonizing someone. The weak, that includes most of them, vote according to the party dictates as that may keep them in good stead with their leadership. So many lies come out of their mouths it appears they don't accept the fact that there will be a JUDGMENT DAY. Their votes on many issues prove that God has NO place in their lives. Maybe they expect a last minute reprieve. God said there is a point of no return, a point when an individual has done so much harm intentionally that he or she is lost forever.

These are adults who know the difference from right and wrong, the difference from what is right or wrong for our country. They know that the laws they pass are either right or wrong. Take Obamacare for example, President Obama has issued 38 changes to the law without congressional approval. How wrong can a law be? Americans vote to put people into positions expecting them to pass laws that are good for our country. Do the Washington elite politicians intentionally deceive the American people? Do the politicians say one thing and then do the opposite? More Americans are waking up to the lies that are being told to them. The question is do most Americans have enough experience to tell when they are being lied to? What does deception look like? A good example of deception is the story of Austria in this book. Is there a comparison to Nazi Germany what Harry Reid, Eric Holder, Dick Durbin, Chuck Shummer, Nancy Pelosi, and other Democratic Party members are carrying on in their goal of transforming America into a socialist country? They are following and obeying the DICTATES of their leader Barack

Obama. During the days of Adolf Hitler, his team of followers loyally followed him. The party loyalty and the goal surpasses the good of the people and in the end the good of the country. The goal of the Democratic Party is socialism, an equality that every person, except for the elite ruling class, has the same stuff. The ruling class then dictates what people can have, what people can say, and what people can believe. Socialism is like Progressivism and Socialism accomplished is Communism.

And it's not only the Democratic Party. Have you listened to Speaker of the House John Boehner? He talks like he is a conservative. He portrays himself to the public as a hard nosed conservative, but he is all about image. Reality check his voting record. He has caved into Obama almost every time. He appears to not have a backbone or behind closed doors he is in cahoots with him. Boehner treats conservative members of his own party harsher than he treats Obama. Boehner has the authority to call for a special investigator to investigate the Obama scandals like

Benghazi or the IRS, but has refused until just recently with the Benghazi fiasco. Did Boehner intentionally wait too long in calling for the special investigator as the odds are there isn't enough time before this Congress ends in December 2014?

Then there is the power of the news media. The power of the news media is AWESOME! The news needs to be OBJECTIVE, but when an experienced and influential reporter like Barbara Walters says she thought Barack Obama was the next MESSIAH one has to question what is presented to the American people.

"The heart of the wise inclines to the right, but the heart of fool to the left."

Ecclesiastes 10:2

Charlie Reese has been a journalist for 49 years. He is retiring and this is his last column, a column for the Orlando Sentinel.

This is about as clear and easy to understand as it can be. The article below is completely neutral, neither anti-Republican or anti-Democrat. Charlie Reese has hit the nail directly on the head, defining clearly who it is that in the final analysis must assume responsibility for the judgments made that impact each one of us every day.

545 vs 300,000,000 People

by Charlie Reese

Politicians are the only people in the world who create problems and then campaign against them.

Have you ever wondered, if both the Democrats and the Republicans are against deficits, WHY do we have deficits?

Have you ever wondered, if all the politicians are against inflation and high taxes, WHY do we have inflation and high taxes?

You and I don't propose a federal budget. The President does.

You and I don't have the Constitutional authority to vote on appropriations. The House of Representatives does.

You and I don't write the tax code, Congress does.

You and I don't set fiscal policy, Congress does.

You and I don't control monetary policy, the Federal Reserve Bank does.

One hundred senators, 435 congressmen, one President, and nine Supreme Court justices equates to 545 human beings out of the 300 million are directly, legally, morally, and individually responsible for the domestic problems that plague this country.

I excluded the members of the Federal Reserve Board because that problem was created by the Congress. In 1913, Congress delegated its Constitutional duty to provide a sound currency to a federally chartered, but private, central bank.

I excluded all the special interests and lobbyists for a sound reason. They have no legal authority. They have no ability to coerce a senator, a congressman, or a President to do one cotton-picking thing. I don't care if they offer a politician $1 million dollars in cash.

The politician has the power to accept or reject it. No matter what the lobbyist promises, it is the legislator's responsibility to determines how he votes.

Those 545 human beings spend much of their energy convincing you that what they did is not their fault. They cooperate in this common con regardless of party.

What separates a politician from a normal human being is an excessive amount of gall. No normal human being would have the gall of a speaker, who stood up and criticized the President for creating deficits. The President can only propose a budget. He cannot force the Congress to accept it.

The Constitution, which is the supreme law of the land, gives sole responsibility to the House of Representatives for originating and approving appropriations and taxes. Who is the speaker of the house? John Boehner. He is the leader of the majority. He and his fellow House members, not the President, can approve any budget they want. If the President vetoes it, they can pass it over his veto if they agree to.

It seems inconceivable to me that a nation of 300 million people cannot replace 545 people who stand convicted -- by present facts -- of incompetence and irresponsibility. I can't think of a single domestic problem that is not traceable directly to those 545 people. When you fully grasp the plain truth that 545 people exercise the power of the federal government, then it must follow that what exists is what they want to exist.

If the tax code is unfair, it is because they want it unfair.

If the budget is in the red, it's because they want it in the red.

If the Army & Marines are in Iraq and Afghanistan, it's because they want them in Iraq and Afghanistan.

If they do not receive social security but are on an elite retirement plan not available to the people, it's because they want it that way.

There are no insoluble problems.

Do not let these 545 people shift the blame to bureaucrats, whom they hire and whose jobs they can abolish; to lobbyists, whose gifts and advice they can reject; to regulators, to whom they give the power to regulate and from whom they can take this power. Above all, do not let them con you into the belief that there exists disembodied mystical forces like "the economy", "inflation", or "politics" that prevent them from doing what they take an oath to do.

Those 545 people, and they alone, are responsible.

They, and they alone, have the power.

They, and they alone, should be held accountable by the people who are their bosses.

Provided the voters have the gumption to manage their own employees.

We should vote all of them out of office and clean up their mess!

The above was Charlie Reese's final column.

A POEM:

Tax his land,

Tax his bed,

Tax the table,

At which he's fed.

Tax his tractor,

Tax his mule,

Teach him taxes,

Are the rule.

Tax his work,

Tax his pay,

He works for

peanuts anyway!

Tax his cow,

Tax his goat,

Tax his pants

Tax his coat.

Tax his ties,

Tax his shirt,

Tax his work,

Tax his dirt.

Tax his tobacco,

Tax his drink,

Tax him if he

Tries to think.

Tax his cigars,

Tax his beers,

If he cries

Tax his tears.

Tax his car,

Tax his gas,

Find other ways

To tax his ass.

Tax all he has,

Then let him know,

That you won't be done
Till he has no dough.

When he screams and hollers,
Then tax him some more,
Tax him till
He's good and sore.

Then tax his coffin,
Tax his grave,
Tax the sod in
Which he's laid.

Put these words,
Upon his tomb,
Taxes drove me
to my doom.

When he's gone,
Do not relax,
It's time to apply
The inheritance tax.

None of the following taxes existed 100 years ago, and our nation was the most prosperous in the world. We had absolutely no national debt, had the largest middle class in the world, and Mom stayed home to raise the kids.

What in the heck happened? Politicians!

1. Accounts Receivable Tax

2. Building Permit Tax

3. Cigarette Tax

4. Corporate Income Tax

5. Dog License Tax

6. Excise Tax

7. Federal Income Tax

8. Federal Unemployment Tax

9. Fishing License Tax

10. Food License Tax

11. Fuel Permit Tax

12. Gasoline Tax

13. Gross Receipts Tax

14. Hunting License Tax

15. Inheritance Tax

16. Liquor Tax

17. Luxury Taxes

18. Marriage License Tax

19. Medicare Tax

20. Personal Property Tax

21. Property Tax

22. Real Estate Tax

23. Service Charge Tax

24. Social Security Tax

25. Road Usage Tax

26. Recreational Vehicle Tax

27. Sales Tax

28. School Tax

29. State Income Tax

30. State Unemployment Tax

31. Telephone Federal Excise Tax

32. Telephone Federal Universal Service Fee Tax

33. Telephone Federal, State, and Local Surcharge Taxes

34. Utility Taxes

35. Vehicle License Registration Tax

36. Vehicle Sales Tax

37. Watercraft Registration Tax

38. Well Permit Tax

39. Workers Compensation Tax

BILLY GRAHAM'S PRAYER FOR OUR NATION

Heavenly Father, we come before You today to ask Your forgiveness and to seek Your direction and guidance. We know Your Word says, "Woe to those who call evil good," but that is exactly what we have done. We have lost our spiritual equilibrium and reversed our values. We have exploited the poor and called it the lottery. We have rewarded laziness and called it welfare. We have killed our unborn and called it choice. We have shot abortionists and called it justifiable. We have neglected to discipline our children and called it building self esteem. We have abused power and called it politics. We have coveted our neighbor's possessions and called it ambition. We have polluted the air with profanity and pornography and called it freedom of expression. We have ridiculed the time -honored values of our forefathers and called it enlightenment. Search us, Oh God, and know our hearts today; cleanse us from sin and set us free. Amen!

With the Lord's help, may this prayer sweep over our nation and wholeheartedly become our desire so that we once again can be called "One nation under God."

OUR FIRST RIGHT: RELIGIOUS LIBERTY

The following was written by Archbishop Charles J. Chaput, O.F.M., Cap

The following remarks by Archbishop Charles Chaput were submitted to the United States Commission on Civil Rights and published March 25, 2013 on Public Discourse

My remarks today are purely my own. But they're shaped by twenty-five years as a Catholic bishop and the social and religious ministries that such work involves; ministries that serve not just Catholics, but the much larger public and common good.

I also served for three years as a Commissioner with the United States Commission on International

Religious Freedom. That experience confirmed for me the unique role that religious faith, religious believers, and religious communities play in genuine human development. It also taught me the importance of religious liberty both abroad and in our country.

Simply put, religious freedom is a fundamental natural right and first among our civil liberties. And I believe this fact is borne out by the priority protection it specifically enjoys, along with freedom of expression, in the Constitution's First Amendment.

I'd like to make four brief points.

Here's my first point : RELIGIOUS FAITH AND PRACTICE ARE OUR CORNERSTONES OF THE AMERICAN EXPERIENCE. It's worth recalling that James Madison, John Adams, John Carroll, John Jay, George Washington, Alexander Hamilton, Benjamin Franklin, Thomas Jefferson, -- in fact, nearly all the American Founders -- saw religious faith as vital to the life of a free people. They believed that liberty and happiness grow organically out of virtue. And virtue needs grounding in religious faith.

To put it another way: At the heart of the American model of public life is an essentially religious vision of man, government, and God. This model has given us a free, open, and non-sectarian society marked by an astonishing variety of cultural and religious expressions. But our system's success does not result from the procedural mechanisms our Founders put in place. Our system works PRECISELY because of the moral assumptions that undergird it. And those moral assumptions have a RELIGIOUS grounding.

When the Founders talked about religion, they meant something much more demanding than a vague "spirituality." The distinguished scholar Harold Berman showed that the Founders -- though they had differing views about religious faith among themselves -- understood religion positively as "both belief in God and belief in an after-life of reward for virtue, and punishment for sin." In other words, religion MATTERED -- personally and socially. It was more than a private preference. It made people live differently and live better. And therefore people's faith was assured to have broad implications, including the social, economic, and political kind.

This leads me to my second point: FREEDOM OF RELIGION IS MORE THAN FREEDOM OF WORSHIP. The right to worship is a necessary but not a sufficient part of religious liberty. For most religious believers, and certainly for Christians, faith requires community. It begins in worship, but it also demands preaching, teaching, and service; in other words, active engagement with society. Faith is always personal but never private. And it involves more than prayer at home and Mass on Sunday -- although these things are vitally important. Real faith always bears fruit in public witness and public action. Otherwise it's just empty words.

The Founders saw the value of publicly engaged religious faith because they inherited its legacy and experienced its formative influence themselves. They created a nation designed in advance to depend on the moral convictions of religious believers, and to welcome their active role in public life.

Here's my third point: THREATS AGAINST RELIGIOUS FREEDOM IN OUR COUNTRY ARE NOT IMAGINARY OR OVERSTATED. THEY'RE HAPPENING RIGHT NOW. THEY'RE IMMEDIATE, SERIOUS, AND REAL. Last year religious liberty advocates won a significant and appropriate Supreme Court victory in the Hosanna-Tabor v. EEOC decision. But what was stunning even to the justices in that case was the disregard for traditional constitutional understandings of religious freedom shown by the government's arguments against the Lutheran church and school. Hosanna-Tabor is not an isolated case. It belongs to a pattern of government coercion that includes the current administration's HHS mandate, which violates the religious identity and mission of many religiously affiliated or inspired public ministries; interfering with the conscience rights of medical providers, private employers, and individual citizens; and attacks on the policies, hiring practices, and tax statuses of religious charities and ministries.

Why is this hostility happening? I believe much of it links to Catholic and other religious teaching on the dignity of life and human sexuality. Catholic moral convictions about abortion, contraception, the purpose of sexuality, and the nature of marriage are rooted not just in revelation, but also in reason and natural law. Human beings have a nature that's not just the product of accident or culture, but inherent, universal, and rooted in permanent truths knowable to reason.

This understanding of the human person is the grounding of the entire American experiment. If human nature is not much more than modeling clay, and no permanent nature exists by the hand of the Creator, then natural, unalienable rights obviously can't exist. And no human "rights" can finally claim priority over the interests of the state.

The problem, as law scholar, Gerard Bradley points out, is that critics of religious faith tend to reduce all of these moral convictions to an expression of subjective beliefs. And if they're purely subjective beliefs, then -- so the critics argue -- they can't be rationally defended. And because they're rationally indefensible, they should be treated as a form of prejudice. In effect, two thousand years of moral experience, moral reasoning, and religious conviction become a species of bias. And arguing against same-sex "marriage" thus amounts to religiously blessed homophobia.

There's more, though. When religious belief is redefined downward to a kind of private bias, then the religious identity of institutional ministries has no public value -- other than the utility of getting credulous people to do good things. So exempting Catholic adoption agencies, for example, from placing children with gay couples becomes a concession to private prejudice. And concessions to private prejudice feed bigotry and hurt the public. Or so the reasoning goes. This is how moral teaching and religious belief end up being branded as hate speech.

Here's my fourth and final point: FROM THE BEGINNING, BELIEVERS -- ALONE AND IN COMMUNITIES -- HAVE SHAPED AMERICAN HISTORY SIMPLY BY TRYING TO LIVE THEIR FAITH IN THE WORLD. WE NEED TO REALIZE THAT AMERICA'S FOUNDING DOCUMENTS ASSUME AN IMPLICITLY RELIGIOUS ANTHROPOLOGY -- AN IDEA OF HUMAN NATURE, NATURE'S GOD, AND NATURAL RIGHTS -- THAT MANY OF OUR LEADERS NO LONGER REALLY SHARE. WE IGNORE THAT UNHAPPY FACT AT OUR OWN EXPENSE.

The following are the author's notes from a sermon by Pastor Dr. Charles Stanley delivered on July 4, 2010.

The title was "Turning the Tide". It expressed Pastor Stanley's concern about our nation.

1. Our country's debt is causing a financial crisis.

2. Our country is divided.

3. The government is causing increasing taxation.

4. The government is spreading our wealth.

5. The government is not responsible to take care of us, but to protect us.

6. We have high unemployment.

7. The government is moving America in the direction of socialism. Socialism is defined as the government controls all production and distribution of things.

This causes no motivation to work, no reward in working.

8. The government is causing confusion, corruption, and silencing the church.

9. Marriage is between a man and a woman. Marriage is the foundation of the family and family is the foundation of our country.

AN EXAMPLE OF THE POWER OF PRAYER

President Ronald Reagan initiated talks with General Secretary Gorbachev of the Soviet Union. Reagan and Gorbachev had four meetings between 1985 and 1988. These talks led to the possibility of Reagan believing Gorbachev became serious about arms control and further reforms. Reagan was right. On June 12, 1987 President Ronald Reagan said, "General Secretary Gorbachev, if you seek peace, if you seek prosperity for the Soviet Union and Eastern Europe, if you seek liberalization, come here to this gate! Mr. Gorbachev, open this gate!, Mr. Gorbachev TEAR DOWN THIS WALL! "

A little known fact that most people don't know is that the people of Leipzig, Germany got involved. Leipzig is located 93 miles south of Berlin.

A brief history of Leipzig and its people. Leipzig, Germany was an industrial city before World War II. The city's Mayor, from 1930 to 1937. was Carl Friedrich Goerdeler, was a noted opponent of the Nazi regime in Germany. He fought against the Nazis until he was forced to resign in 1937.

The city was heavily damaged by Allied bombing during World War II. The Allied ground advance into Germany reached Leipzig in late April 1945. The U.S. 2nd Infantry Division and the U.S. 69th Infantry division fought into the city on April 18th. The U.S. turned the city over to the Red Army as it pulled back from the "line of contact" with Soviet forces in July 1945 to the predesignated occupation zone boundaries. Leipzig became one of the major cities of East Germany.

Inspired by President Ronald Reagan's speech for peace, reforms, and liberty, the people of Leipzig began peaceful demonstrations against the East Germany government, the German Democratic

Republic (GDR). on September 4,1989 after meeting for prayers for peace at St. Nicholas Church, a small group demonstrated. Led by parson Christian Fuhrer they met every Monday to pray for peace and then demonstrated. Safe in the knowledge that the Lutheran Church supported their resistance, many dissatisfied East German citizens gathered in the court of the church, and non-violent demonstrations began in order to demand rights such as the freedom to travel to foreign countries and to elect a democratic government.

By October 9, 1989, just after the 40th anniversary celebrations of the GDR, what had begun as a few hundred gathers at the St. Nicholas Church swelled to more than 70,000, all united in peaceful opposition to the regime. The most famous chant became "wir sind das Volk!, (We are the People!), reminding their rulers that a democratic republic has to be ruled by the people, not by an undemocratic party claiming to represent them.

Although some demonstrators were arrested, the threat of large scale intervention by security forces never materialized as local leaders, without precise orders from East Berlin, and surprised by the unexpectedly high number of citizens, shied away from causing a possible massacre, ordering retreat of their forces. The next week in Leipzig, October 16, 1989, 120,000 showed up, with military units again being held on standby in the vicinity. The next week, the number more than doubled to 320,000 people. This pressure led to the fall of the Berlin Wall on November 9, 1989, marking the imminent fall of the socialist GDR regime.

The demonstrations eventually ended in March 1990, around the time of the first free multi-party elections for the parliament that paved the way to German reunification.

THE PRAYERS OF THE PEOPLE OF LEIPZIG PLAYED A SIGNIFICANT ROLE IN INSTIGATING THE FALL OF COMMUNISM IN EASTERN

EUROPE, THROUGH EVENTS WHICH TOOK PLACE IN AND AROUND ST. NICHOLAS CHURCH. THE EFFORTS LED TO THE BERLIN WALL COMING DOWN AND THE REUNIFICATION OF GERMANY.

The Cold War was officially declared over at the Malta Summit on December 3, 1989 and two years later, the Soviet Union collapsed.

A DOCTOR'S STORY

This is a pretty neat story from a doctor and an interesting thing that few of us know. It's brief, so please read to the end, you will be AMAZED!

A couple of days ago I was running (I use that term very loosely) on my treadmill, watching a DVD sermon by Louie Giglio. I was BLOWN AWAY!

He (Louie) was talking about how inconceivably BIG our GOD is. How He spoke the universe into being.

How He breathes stars out of His mouth that are huge raging balls of fire, Etc, Etc, Then he went on to speak of how this star breathing, universe creating God ALSO knitted our human bodies together with amazing detail and wonder. At this point I am loving it, (fascinating from a medical standpoint). And I was remembering how I was constantly amazed during medical school as I learned more and more about God's handiwork. I remember so many times thinking, How can ANYONE deny that a CREATOR did all of this?

Louie went on to talk about how we can trust that the God who created all this, also has the power to hold it all together when things seem to be falling apart, how our loving Creator is also our sustainer.

And then I lost my breath. And it wasn't because I was running on my treadmill, either!

It was because Louie started to talk about laminin. I knew about laminin. Here is how Wikipedia describes them: Laminins are a family of proteins that are an integral part of the structural scaffolding of basement membranes in almost every animal tissue. You see, Laminins are what hold us together LITERALLY. They are cell adhesion molecules. They are what hold one cell of our bodies to the next cell. Without them, we would literally fall apart. And I knew all this already. But what I didn't know is what they LOOKED LIKE. But now I do. And I have thought about it a thousand times since. Here is what the structure of laminin looks like. And this is not a Christian portrayal of it. If you look up laminin in any scientific/ medical piece of literature, this is what you will see.

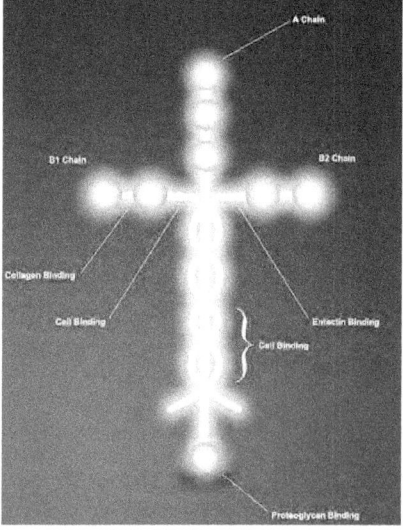

Now tell me that our God is not the coolest! Amazing! The glue that holds us together, ALL of us, Is in the shape of the cross. Immediately Colossians 1:15-17 comes to mind.

"He is the image of the invisible God, the firstborn over all creation. For by Him all things were created; things in heaven and on earth, visible and invisible, whether thrones or powers or rulers or authorities. All things were created by Him and for Him. He is before all things, and in Him all things HOLD TOGETHER."

Call me crazy. I just think that is very, very, cool. Thousands of years before the world knew anything about laminin, the Apostle Paul penned these words in his writing of the Colossians. And now we see that from a very LITERAL STANDPOINT, WE ARE HELD TOGETHER, ONE CELL TO ANOTHER, BY THE CROSS.

You would never in a quadrillion years convince me that is anything other than the mark of a Creator who knew EXACTLY what laminin "glue" would look like long before Adam breathed his first breath!

The above story were the comments of a doctor. A doctor STUDIES every part of the human body in medical school. If a doctor is so AMAZED of how our bodies are created shouldn't everyone else?

GENESIS CHAPTER 1 -- IN THE BEGINNING GOD CREATED THE HEAVEN AND EARTH. If you read all of chapter one of Genesis you will see how God created the earth and everything in it.

The END TIME

It appears more and more people are talking about the END TIME. A number of pastors who not only have read the Bible, but actually studied it, are telling anyone who will listen that ALL the signs mentioned in the Bible have been met or are presently put in motion. Why should we be concerned about the END TIME? Because the END TIME is the END of the age. The world as we know it will NOT exist anymore. It will be destroyed! This time by fire!. Yes, the fire that comes from war and nuclear bombs. Anyone who knows anything about nuclear weapons knows that enough of them going off can destroy our planet. And anyone who knows the fanatic mind of those who want to conquer other people, also knows the passionate mind of those who want to defend themselves. One nuclear bomb will lead to another and another and another, etc. This time the weapons of mass destruction will be fatal. The END. The END of everything! Doomsday!

The enemies of Israel are growing and getting stronger. These enemies have stated over and over again and again they will destroy Israel. This time they will succeed! The United States of America will not be able to prevent it from happening. The Bible is clear once Israel has been defeated it's ALL OVER.

What should anyone do? It is time to face reality.

The author's notes from the END TIME sermons of Pastor Ed Young, who is the leading pastor of a mega church in Texas that draws 25,000 people weekly to hear his sermons.

It is time to believe in God. Accept Jesus Christ as YOUR Lord and Savior. Make Jesus the central point of your life. That should become the central fact of your life. Family, job, money, health, pleasure, and happiness SHOULD be secondary to making Jesus first in your life. Jesus, the Lord God should reign in your life!

As Israel is defeated, the SECOND COMING OF JESUS CHRIST will defeat all the enemies. Jesus Christ will reign forever and ever.

But where will you be?

To explain in simple terms, and probably in terms you may never have heard before. Because Jesus Christ ROSE from the grave as He preached, He conquered DEATH. He was and is the Son of God, in fact He was God in the flesh. Jesus Christ conquered DEATH! And He conquered DEATH for ALL of us. Because of that, DEATH IS DEAD! There are three kinds of DEATH. There is PHYSICAL DEATH, there is SPIRITUAL DEATH, and there is ETERNAL DEATH. Physical death everyone dies, except for those who will be alive when Jesus comes. Spiritual death is for everyone who lives in sin. Eternal death is decided at the FINAL JUDGMENT. All will appear in the JUDGMENT seat of Jesus Christ -- for good or bad (evil). The Christians will live with Jesus Christ in

ETERNITY. The rest will live in the fire of HELL in ETERNITY.

The beauty of the FINAL JUDGMENT is that EACH PERSON decides based on their life and the acceptance of Jesus Christ as Lord and Savior where he or she wants to live in ETERNITY. Therefore, we all live, but the only question is where.

WHERE WILL YOU LIVE IN ETERNITY?

For continuity and clarity of the above message, the Bible verses that apply are given here. They are not in any particular order.

1 Thessalonians 4:16-17
For the Lord himself shall descend from heaven with a shout, with the voice of the archangel, and with the trump of God: and the dead in Christ shall rise first; Then we which are alive and remain shall be caught up together with them in the clouds, to meet the Lord in the air: and so shall we be ever with the Lord.

Romans 6:20-23

For when we were the servants of sin, ye were free from righteousness, What fruit had ye then in those things whereof ye are now ashamed? For the end of those things is death. But now being made free from sin, and become servants to God, ye have your fruit unto holiness, and the end everlasting life. For the wages of sin is death; but the gifts of God is eternal life through Jesus Christ our Lord.

1 Corinthians 15:22- 26

For as in Adam all die, even so in Christ shall be made alive. But every man in his own order: Christ the first fruits; afterward they that are Christ's at his coming. Then cometh the end, when he shall have delivered up the kingdom to God, even the Father; when he shall have put down all rulc and all authority and power. For he must reign, till he hath put all enemies under his feet. The last enemy that shall be destroyed is death.

Revelation 19:5-6

And a voice came out of the throne, saying, Praise our God, all ye his servants, and ye that fear him, both small and great. And I heard as it were the voice of a great multitude, and as the voice of many waters, and as the voice of mighty thunderings, saying, Alleluia; for the Lord God omnipotent reigneth.

2 Corinthians 5:10

For we must all appear before the judgment seat of Christ; that every one may receive the things done in HIS (service to God) body, according to that he hath done, whether it be good or bad.

Revelation 10:6

And sware by him that liveth for ever and ever, who created heaven, and the things that therein are, and the earth, and the things that therein are, and the sea, and the things which are therein, that there should be TIME NO LONGER.

Revelation 21:1-8

And I saw a new heaven and a new earth: for the first heaven and the first earth were passed away; and there was no more sea. And I John saw the holy city, new Jerusalem, coming down from God out of heaven, prepared as a bride adorned for her husband. And I heard a great voice out of heaven saying, Behold, the tabernacle of God is with men, and he will dwell with them, and they shall be his people, and God himself shall be with them, and be their God. And God shall wipe away all tears from their eyes; and there shall be no more death, neither sorrow, nor crying, neither shall there be any more pain: for the former things are passed away. And he that sat upon the throne said, Behold, I make all things new. And he said unto me, It is done. I am alpha and Omega, the beginning and the end. I will give unto him that is at thirst of the fountain of the water of life freely. He that overcometh shall inherit all things and I will be his God, and he shall be my son. For the fearful, and unbelieving, and the abominable, and murderers, and whoremongers, and sorcerers, and idolaters, and all liars, shall have their part in the lake which burneth with fire and brimstone: which is the second death.

If you have read the book to this point you know what has happened and is happening. The BOMBS of destruction have been the assaults on our basic values, our basic principles, and our basic Christian beliefs. Why does this matter? It's because our basic values, principles, and Christian beliefs HOLD our country together. The great empires of the past first were destroyed from within before their enemies came and defeated them. Being defeated from within is equal to bombs going off. It is as devastating as bombs actually landing on us. It has the same effect. It serves the same purpose. It weakens us as a country. President Barack Obama and his administration, have created the largest DECEPTION in the history of America as he has almost completed the TRANSFORMATION that he promised in his speeches. But Americans who voted for him assumed the TRANSFORMATION would be good for them and for America. When a large number of the jobs created are part-time jobs that makes paying the monthly bills a great burden. Obama's intentions have become clear to any American who is paying attention to his policies of destruction. Obama has stated that America is NOT a Christian nation, but is a Muslim nation. Do you understand what that implies. And the Democratic Progressive Party is FOLLOWING him like sheep. They are unquestionably putting into action what he dictates. The deception and the lies are truly everywhere. The cover up of all of the scandals by the people of his administration is proof of their commitment to him. There is little transparency. There is even less TRUTH out of this administration.

The author SEEKS THE TRUTH in everything. It is most important to evaluate a person based on character traits, values, principles, and beliefs. Watch what a person does. Talk is cheap, especially for a politician. A political party CAN NOT take the place of God or country. God and country should trump any political party. America does not need a political party that resembles the Nazi Party.

The question is not IF God is on our side, but are we on His side. As Americans' faith in God has dwindled to the point of "almost" no return why should God protect us.

Remember, when the Israelites left God they were on their own and that didn't work out too well. Only when they returned to God did He protect them again. America needs to return to God ASAP.

So far those bombs have been "invisible", non-physical, but as lethal as if they were atomic or nuclear bombs. Only time will tell when the bombs become nuclear.

This book is a WARNING! Our national defense is at its weakest point since not only World War II, but actually World War I.

To survive, you must do what is required of you. You must accept Jesus Christ as your Lord and Savior.

You then must live a life without sin, live a Christian life.

If millions of Americans start living a Christian life, God has promised to take notice. He will once again protect the United States of America.

But, if America does NOT become a Christian nation again this is what will happen.

The stage is being set right now as the conditions are ripe for civil unrest. Civil unrest? It will be the people who feel entitled to everything without working for it AGAINST the people who are working for it. It will be far worse than the American Civil War as our present Obama administration is on the side of the unentitled, the people who don't want to work for it. Plus our other potential enemies, Russia, China, and the Jihad, will take advantage of our weakness and bomb us into the 17th Century. The result will be the USA will no longer exist.

America as we presently know her now will not exist. It will be a new world. The big three, Russia, China, and the Jihad will compromise and establish the United Nations in charge of a one world order. Why? Because the nation that kept fighting for "freedom" has been defeated and the big three believe in a Communist/ Marxist form of government. The United Nations believes in a world without borders, a world without country names that is the cause of national pride and allegiances. They will rename the world with numbers. For example, the United States of America could be called United Nations 140, or UN 140. There will be no more striving for individual success as incentive has been replaced with just a sharing of whatever resources are given by the RULERS.

American women will be living under Sharia law. They will be covered from head to toe, only their eyes will be visible. They won't be worrying about whether they get free contraceptives anymore. The liberal organizations that demanded the government adopt all of the social changes will answer to the new Rulers. This will happen until Jesus returns.

Then Jesus returns! The Big three are defeated! The world is renewed! Jesus rules the world!

The USA, the United States of America, is NOT mentioned in the last Book of the Bible, the Revelation. Does that mean we have been defeated before the END TIME just as it is written above?

FINAL THOUGHTS

It is important to know what our Founding Fathers intended as they established America. America is to be a nation where any and all laws would be based on God's laws. The law could not contradict any of God's principles. The Founding Fathers wrote extensively about this.

America's first Chief Justice of the Supreme Court, John Jay:

"Providence has given to our people the choice of their rulers, and it is the duty, as well as the privilege and interest, of our Christian nation to select and prefer Christians for their rulers. He also expressed a belief that the moral precepts of Christianity were necessary for good government, saying, "No human society has ever been able to maintain order and freedom, both cohesiveness and liberty apart from the moral precepts of the Christian Religion. Should our

Republic ever forget this fundamental precept of governance, we will then, be surely doomed."

Four U.S. Supreme Court cases describing America as a "Christian Nation", (1844-1931).

In 1892, Supreme Court Justice David Brewer writing in "Church of the Holy Trinity vs U.S. case", the unanimous Supreme Court decision which has never been overturned, held as a matter of law, fact, and history that THIS IS A CHRISTIAN NATION because our laws and public institutions are founded on Biblical principles from the Old and New Testaments. From the discovery of this continent to the present hour, there is a single voice making this affirmation. We find everywhere a clear recognition of the same truth this is a Christian nation."

The four Supreme Court decisions describing America as a Christian nation are: Vidal vs Girard's Executors (1844), Church of Jesus Christ of Latter Day Saints vs United States (1890), Church of the Holy

Trinity vs United States (1892), and United States vs MacIntosh (1931).

In the 1844 case, Vidal vs Girard's Executors, the Supreme Court held in a unanimous opinion read by Supreme Court Justice Joseph Story: "Christianity is not to be maliciously and openly reviled and blasphemed against, to the annoyance of believers or the injury of the public."

Joseph Story served on the U.S. Supreme Court for 33 years, 1812 -1845. He wrote "nine commentaries on the law" which have been celebrated as scholarly work and a foundation for many law cases. Story is considered the "Father of American Jurisprudence"

Throughout this book you have read that our Founding Fathers embraced Christianity and gave God the credit for their success in the founding of America. The American Revolution lasted 8 years, 1776 - 1783. If there ever was an INDISPENSABLE MAN it was George Washington. If you have studied the founding of America you surely would agree. Washington was a Christian man. One public example of this, George Washington was on his knees in the snow at Valley Forge praying to God. When God starts something He will finish it with the outcome He wants. It was miracle after miracle over 8 years that Washington even survived as he led the charge on his horse in many battles. Only because God's hand was on Washington did he survive to lead our country. One example, was when a British officer, Major Ferguson, who was a sharp shooter, had his rifle's sights on George Washington who was standing with his back turned in a group of men several hundred yards away, that Ferguson decided not to shoot. Ferguson said, "he didn't want to shoot anyone who wasn't engaged in a battle." Ferguson had no idea that his target was George Washington. As the men walked into the trees he realized his target had been Washington. By the GRACE OF GOD, George Washington lived. AND BY THE GRACE OF GOD AMERICA WAS FOUNDED.

Another example of God's Providence on George Washington was during the fierce battles of the French Indian War of July 1755. The French were fighting the British. George Washington was a colonel in the British army. During the battles the British were almost all killed. When Washington returned to his base, he took off his jacket, he found 4 bullet holes through it but not a single bullet touched him. He had horses shot from under him. George Washington said, "I now exist and appear in the land of the living by the miraculous care of Providence that protected me beyond all human expectation."

PSALM 33:12

BLESSED IS THE NATION WHOSE GOD IS THE LORD;, AND THE PEOPLE WHOM HE HATH CHOSEN FOR HIS OWN INHERITANCE.

The First Amendment to our Constitution

Clearly, neither the word "separation", "church", nor "state" is found in any part of the first Amendment. In fact, that phrase appears in NO governmental founding document.

The First Amendment barred the federal government from interfering with or limiting the peoples' public religious expressions. The Free Exercise Clause of the First Amendment required the federal government to protect, rather than suppress public religious expressions. The phrase, "separation of church and state" appeared in a PRIVATE LETTER written by Thomas Jefferson some 13 years after the First Amendment was written. Jefferson wrote to the Danbury Baptists on January 1, 1802, "assuring them that their free exercise of religion was indeed an inalienable right and would not be meddled with by the federal government because there was a "wall of separation between church and state" that would prevent the government from interfering with or hindering religious activities."

But in 1947 the courts made a radical change. In "Everson vs Board of Education" the Supreme Court cited only Jefferson's "separation" metaphor, ignoring the rest of his letter and its clear context. It therefore boldly announced a new standard:

The First amendment has erected a wall between church and state. That wall must be kept high and impregnable. We could not approve the slightest breach."

So without ANY LEGAL PRECEDENT the Supreme Court CHANGED the MEANING of the First Amendment. The courts elevated a single phrase from a private letter -- a phrase completely reversed from its original meaning -- above the actual language of the First Amendment itself.

WITHOUT ANY LEGAL AUTHORITY THE SUPREME COURT JUSTICES IMPOSED THEIR WILL ON THE AMERICAN PEOPLE. ONLY A CONSTITUTIONAL AMENDMENT CAN CHANGE AN EXISTING AMENDMENT. THESE JUSTICES OPENED THE FLOOD GATES OF HELL ON THE AMERICAN PEOPLE.

ABOUT THE AUTHOR

Roger Ewing has a Bachelor's Degree from Bowling Green State University in Ohio. He received a Master's Degree from the University of Southern California and did his PhD work at Arizona State University.

Roger was an Air Force Officer and a Management Consultant for many years. He loves animals, and has rescued approximately 250 Saint Bernard dogs from animal shelters.

Roger has been active in the conservative movement to inform Americans about our Constitution, and what we need to do to preserve our country.